FRANCE
A guide for the independent traveller

FRANCE
A guide for the independent traveller

JOHN P. HARRIS

MACMILLAN

First published 1986 by
PAPERMAC
a division of Macmillan Publishers Limited
4 Little Essex Street London WC2R 3LF
and Basingstoke

Associated companies in Auckland, Delhi, Dublin,
Gaborone, Hamburg, Harare, Hong Kong, Johannesburg,
Kuala Lumpur, Lagos, Manzini, Melbourne, Mexico City,
Nairobi, New York, Singapore and Tokyo

British Library Cataloguing in Publication Data
Harris, John, *1923–*
    France: a guide for the independent traveller
    1. France – Handbooks, manuals, etc.
    I. Title
    914.4'04838   DC17

    ISBN 0-333-39849-1

Typeset by Bookworm Typesetting Ltd, Manchester
Printed in Great Britain by Anchor Brendon Ltd, Tiptree, Essex

For Anne and Arthur

Contents

Acknowledgements

This book owes its existence and any merits it may possess to my wife Sophie.

For information, suggestions and other help I am grateful to Her Majesty's Consular Service, Harold Chapman, Nick Chapman, Bill and Bouton Garrad, Dominique Giganté (Gîtes de France), Pauline Hallam (FNTO, London), Ernest Lee, Mark Lintott, Caroline McCarthy (SNCF, London), Claire Parry, Padgett and Gretchen Payne, Henri Poujol, Barbara Proctor, Judith Rothchild, André Ruas, Frank and Joan Sargeant, and George and Barbara Wolstenholme. As for the faults in these pages, they are all my own work.

I am grateful to the editors of *The Times* and of *SHE*, where fragments of this book first appeared.

Introduction

For sun, candy floss and cheap drinks Spain is perhaps best. A lolly-stick's throw along the concrete, *Sauerkraut mit Eisbein* steams all day in the take-aways, near the place where they do the *echte Hollandse pannekoeken*. Apart from waiters, pick-pockets, pseudo-folkdancers and others who do well out of tourism, the natives have fled.

France too can cater for Saudi and Texan oil sheiks and parties from Scunthorpe. It has a lot of sights to be *done*, as well. I would not want to put anyone off going up the Eiffel Tower once, poking his nose into the Place du Tertre at Montmartre and perhaps buying a postcard at Mont-Saint-Michel and a plastic gargoyle at Carcassonne. But this book is for the independent traveller and the short-stay citizen.

The French have a conservative tendency, irritating to some ('Frogs are slightly better than Huns or Wops, but abroad is unutterably bloody and foreigners are fiends,' says Uncle Matthew in Nancy Mitford's *The Pursuit of Love*), to think that their way of doing things is the only proper, or civilised, or conceivable way. My wife Sophie and I spent many holidays in

France, usually camping when the children were small and we were hard up. Now we live there. We don't think the French way is the only way. There is a lot to be said for the British way, and we would be pleased to divide our time between the Midi and London if someone gave us a Knightsbridge flat and £50,000 a year spending money. But we are quite happy to have gone native in France, and we have grown fond of our French neighbours. The French way is all right.

Two things about France, to start with. One is that it is bigger than Britain, with about the same population. Travel – real travel, with surprises, many of them agreeable – is still possible on its vast network of secondary roads. In summer Dartmoor is crowded with the cars of solitude seekers. Where we live, the moors (*les causses, la garrigue*) reveal in mid-August an occasional car and a picnicking family or two, and one feels like stopping for a chat. In April there are acres of wild daffodils and such solitude that I am glad, after a couple of hours, to wend my way down the valley to a friendly village and rediscover the pleasures of human society.

And then Britain and France remain so different, even today, when Muzak and fish fingers are the same from Reykjavík to Wagga Wagga. This, since the countries are near, is convenient for citizens of both, when they feel in need of a radical and (one hopes) refreshing change. France is easier to adapt to: it is (superficially at least) a more open country. Compare for instance the pub and the café. The interior of the pub is invisible from the street: you have to go right inside to see if it is the sort of place you want to spend the next hour in. Most of my favourite pubs are ones I've been introduced to by a friend. But the café is wide open, and probably has a terrace. At a glance one sees if it is packed with *la jeunesse* deafening itself with Franco-mid-Atlantic rock, or American ladies airing their poor feet and calling for milk, or housewives with shopping baskets gossiping after the weekly market, or students revising their dissertations over an economical coffee....

It didn't take us long to learn how to profit from some of the best things in French life – to know the ropes. Those ropes are the subject of this book. I am not qualified to write about France except on a fairly superficial level: I am not an historian or a geographer or a sociologist, just someone who has been going there on and off all his life and now finds it a convenient, comfortable, interesting, usually cheerful and often beautiful place to live in.

Chapter 1

The French

Generalisations about national character are – to generalise – largely bosh. Sophie and I get on well with some people, less well with others. We know a fair number of English, Scottish, French, Dutch, American and Italian people whom we find absolute stinkers, and fortunately a much greater number whom we love, admire or respect. The colour of their passports has nothing to do with the matter.

However, traditions and habits of mind sometimes coincide vaguely with national boundaries. I hope that the reader will find a stratum of helpful truth here, but it takes all sorts to make a world and even a country, so you never know.

'The French are individualists' is a cliché. To quote from an earlier book of mine:

> don't be a unit, be a human being, and get on the personal level as soon as possible ... French bureaucracy has a fearsome reputation, but if only one can find the person who matters, and become a person to him or her, difficulties melt away ... If I go to a big garage just before closing time I

may get the brush-off, but if I go to a small garage, just after closing time and explain what a service they would render me if they would help me on my weary way, I shall probably be fixed up, and given all sorts of good advice into the bargain; the man and I are reacting at the human level. If you don't want to shake hands with ordinary people and at least pretend to take an interest in what makes them tick, avoid France, especially rural France. You may save time elsewhere and no doubt get what you pay for. But no more.

Four more years of happy living have gone by, and I still like the French.

Sociability and privacy

The temporary citizen, especially in a village *gîte*, will find that the locals are interested in him, his habits and tastes, the number and ages of his children, and so forth. They love to talk, and often to listen. But they are great respecters of privacy. Villagers do not pop freely into one another's houses, drinking casual cups of coffee and borrowing half a pound of sugar. They need a neutral place in which to socialise. In a village this will be a bench in the sun or the shade; elsewhere, perhaps a café – anywhere outside the private lair. We have ten French casual acquaintances for every British or American one, here in our little corner, but we share pot-luck meals with the latter; they drop in on us and we on them. Our French villager friends are timid about entering our (very simple) house. If they want to ask us about something they prefer to chat on the doorstep. They penetrate our house, and we penetrate theirs, when specifically invited: *apéritifs*, or dinner, or something else – and the occasion is rather formal. That is how they behave among themselves, too. If you want to keep yourself to yourself the French will let you, but they don't want to be stand-offish.

If you have rented a *gîte* your landlord may well pay you the compliment of inviting you in for a drink. A small point here: a recent writer says: 'You will probably be sat round a table as the host dispenses his homemade wine, a sweet sherry-type brew of great potency. There is no choice.' Nonsense. Do, of course, accept the invitation – it would cause deep offence if you didn't. But there is no need to drink any 'sweet sherry-type brew' if you don't want to. French people, especially older village ones, seem rather proud of their frailties, such as finding that alcohol outside meal-times, or wine unmixed with water, or coffee after 4 p.m., disagrees with them (*je ne supporte pas le* ——, *hélas* – 'I can't take ——, alas') and a *jus de fruit* or a glass of mineral water (*un verre d'eau minérale*) will always be forthcoming if you ask, and will satisfy protocol if you are wary of the *apéritif*. The ceremony is the thing. Ask your landlord back, another day, for a reciprocal ceremony; offer the whisky you bought on the boat, but make sure you have a bottle of *eau minérale* in the fridge, and don't be upset if that's what he wants.

Manners

Whether in the inmost depths of their souls the French are politer than the British is a question I shall not venture upon. On the superficial level there are politenesses which should be observed if one is not to seem grossly rude. One simply must say *Bonjour madame/mademoiselle/monsieur/mesdames/messieurs/ messieurs-dames* much more often than would be thought necessary. And *merci, madame* (etc.), and *au revoir* (etc.), optionally replacing the last by *bon appétit* within half an hour of meal-times. On going through a door a fair amount of *après vous*-ing is compulsory, with *pardon* if one goes first, momentarily turning one's back. The simplest and least educated of French people do these things.

If you are in a *gîte* in a village, and if your French is up to it, it will increase your reputation as a civilised human being if you tell temporary acquaintances what you are doing, or on the point of doing, even if it seems obvious. *Nous allons à la mer . . . nous nous promenons . . . je lave la voiture . . .* Rural French people talk about the weather even more than the British do.

Il fait beau, n'est-ce pas? Such simple noises must be made; their purpose is to show that one does not regard people as farmyard animals, lumps of stone or just invisible. If you have not a word of French, learn *bonjour* quickly, and smile. Even in Paris, except in the rush hour.

Acquaintances' hands, if proffered, should be shaken daily on meeting and on parting. The French are quick on the draw; failure to respond will cause grave concern.

When introduced, it is safe to declare that you are *enchanté* (*monsieur, madame* or *mademoiselle*); but males introduced to ladies who might not object to being thought old enough to be their mothers should offer *mes hommages, madame*.

THE FRENCH AS LETTER-WRITERS

Ordinary French people may seem verbally politer than their British opposite numbers, but such punctiliousness is confined to the spoken language. They hate writing letters. The British will scribble short notes and send them by return of post. The majority of the French are afraid to put pen to paper. If writing to an office, one is more likely to get a prompt reply if it can come in the form of a leaflet or the return of one's own letter with *oui, non,* etc., written in the margin.

Do not be offended if French holiday acquaintances do not reply to your letters! They really do, or did, mean to. And it would have been a beautiful letter, with a rough copy made first. But then, so many problems arose. ... If you have learnt French the old-fashioned way, and reached 'A' level standard, you may be far from fluent in speech, but your spelling is better than that of half the population.

On the other hand, the most literate 2 per cent of the population will reply so elegantly that one will be put to shame. Oh, how the French respect the written language! And how they fear it, most of them!

Tipping – le pourboire

Cinema and theatre ushers should be given a franc or two: this is the accepted custom, they rely on it, and protest if you try to deprive them of their due. The odd coin should also be left (in the saucer thoughtfully placed on a table) for lavatory attendants.

Otherwise the situation is as in Britain, or indeed simpler, thanks to the service-charge system. Tip only when you have asked for and received some extra act of service, in cafés, restaurants and hotels. Taxi drivers, as at home, like 10 per cent or more.

Their time-table

British holiday-makers may or may not decide to do things at French times. If they are going to be out of phase, they need to know the local rhythm, so as to avoid surprises and disappointments for themselves and inconvenience for others.

HOURS

The French day starts early. Most people are at work by 8 a.m. (This can lead the French to think the British lazy: French clock time is an hour later than British, so a Parisian businessman may have put in two and a half hours at his desk before his London opposite number answers the phone.) A village shop may open at 7 a.m., so that people can go there before they leave for work. In the Midi, 6 a.m. will not be too early to spray the vineyards while it is still cool. Banks are usually open by 9 a.m.

No coffee break. At 12 p.m., half the day's work is done. Most activity stops for *le déjeuner* (called *le dîner* in the country) until 2 p.m. – or until a good deal later, in the Midi. The village shop that opened at 7 a.m. might re-open 4–7 p.m. The vineyard owner who started at 6 a.m. will have knocked off by 11 a.m.; then he will put in three or four hours in the cool of the evening.

People go home to lunch if they can. It follows that if you want to catch your Frenchman at home, 12.30 p.m. is a good time. In the small ads in the local paper it says *tél HR*, short for *téléphonez aux heures des repas* – phone at meal-times. That means between 12 p.m. and 2 p.m., or around 8 p.m. Lunch is a serious business, almost sacred, so *Pardon de vous déranger* is polite (*déranger* is not to derange, but to be a nuisance). Three in the afternoon is not such a good time; your Frenchman, if not at work, may be catching up on his sleep with a well-earned siesta (in the Midi, if he works in the open, and if he is his own boss).

Restaurants open their doors at midday. One might get served at 1.30 p.m., but perhaps not in small places.

'High tea' is unknown. (French students of English often think that this expression means a very elegant afternoon tea, as served at Claridge's or the Dorchester.) Children and old ladies might have a *goûter* at four or five, but everyone else keeps going on the lunchtime calories. Six is knocking-off time, but later at most shops. *Le dîner* (*le souper* in the country) is around 8 p.m. Cinemas and theatres start at nine or half past. Going out in the evening *pour s'amuser* implies a short night's sleep.

DAYS

Shops tend to open to suit the convenience of the (French) customer, rather than that of their staff. The butcher, the baker and the village *épicerie* are open on Sunday mornings, *naturellement*, though they may close on Mondays. The bank is shut on Saturday and Sunday, but if the local market day is Saturday it will be open then, closing on Monday instead. (This means that customers can actually go to the bank when they need to, quite unlike dear old England.)

A few shops (chemists, sometimes) shut on Saturdays, opening on Mondays. Monday is not a good shopping day, except at supermarkets and hypermarkets.

Museums and art galleries (both are called *musées*, m.) tend to shut on Tuesdays.

Wednesday is a day off from school. They have classes on Saturdays.

Sunday midday is the big time for restaurants. Not,

however, in those towns where the inhabitants get into their cars and drive to restaurants in the country or by the sea; in such towns, restaurants make Sunday their weekly closing day. It will be some other day for the out-of-town places, often Monday or Tuesday (see Michelin for individual restaurants).

THE YEAR

On public holidays (*jours fériés*) big shops, banks, etc., close; small shops may stay open; restaurants as Sunday.

le jour de l'an – New Year's Day
lundi de Pâques – Easter Monday (but not Good Friday)
fête du travail – Labour Day, 1 May
Armistice '45 – VE Day, 8 May
Ascension – Ascension Day (a Thursday, linked to Easter)
lundi de Pentecôte – Whit Monday (linked to Easter)
fête nationale – 'Bastille Day', 14 July
Assomption – Assumption Day, 15 August
Toussaint – All Saints' Day, 1 November
Armistice '18 – Remembrance Day, 11 November
Noël – Christmas Day, 25 December (but not Boxing Day)

If one of these public holidays falls on a normal day off, that is just bad luck; there is no tradition (as yet) of taking another day off instead. On the other hand, there is a growing custom of making *un pont*, a bridge: if *la fête du travail* falls on a Tuesday, for example, Monday may be taken off too. When a *jour férié* approaches it is wise to look at notices on bank doors to see if any bridge-building is planned.

On *jours fériés* establishments in business to give pleasure to the public (theatres, many restaurants, *pâtisseries*, even bakers . . .) tend to open – even on Christmas Day. If a public holiday falls on their normal closing day (*fermeture hebdomadaire*, weekly closing) they may well stay open, and take the following day off. Market days will probably be displaced to avoid a public holiday. When planning visits, excursions or feasts it is prudent to enquire about what may be happening on the day before and the day after a *jour férié,* as well as on the day itself.

French wage-earners get five weeks' paid holiday. They usually take three or four weeks in August, or perhaps July, and the remainder in winter – many go ski-ing, a more classless exercise than in Britain. On the weekend nearest to 1 September *(la rentrée)* everybody goes back to work (traffic jams).

In May, June, September and October the weather can be good; only foreigners are on holiday, and hotel and restaurant keepers are delighted to see them. (November to April have their pleasures, too.)

Chapter 2

Books and guides

There is no shortage of English books about France: her history, geography, literature, art, folk-lore, wines, cooks and politics. Scholars from Ardagh to Zeldin have scrutinised the population. Particular regions have been the object of labours of loving accuracy, while a few nicely illustrated coffee-table books have had their texts hurriedly compiled at second-hand by hacks. Browsing in public libraries and bookshops is recommended for choosing background reading to suit individual tastes and interests.

The term 'guide book' can mean anything from a permanently valuable work on countryside and architecture to a list of selected hotels and restaurants. The last sort can be dangerous. Cathedrals and rivers change slowly if at all, but information on hotels, official regulations and special offers should be up to date. Leaflets and brochures, in French and in English, cost nothing but the postage. Guides that name hotels and restaurants should be the current year's edition. I am writing this book in the hope that much of it will relate to fairly permanent features of the French way of life, but I must ask the reader's pardon if some information proves perishable. For example, I am sure that the French Ministry of Transport will continue its system of signposting recommended secondary roads (see page 48), but it might well get tired of the Red Indian gimmick and drop the name *Bison Futé*. This chapter is about how to get hot news straight from the horse's mouth.

Exploit the French National Tourist Office, at 178 Piccadilly, London W1V 0AL. Every year in January they publish *The Traveller in France*, sent free and post free to all who apply. This is a cheerful magazine-like publication. More valuable is the reference guide that comes with it: several pages of small print, up-to-date facts, special events, festivals, book lists, addresses of specialist travel agents in the UK, and addresses in the UK and France to write to for fuller information about a host of matters (self-catering holidays, regions, working holidays . . .). The Office is open from 9 a.m. to 5 p.m. on weekdays, for enquiries and for collecting leaflets.

Next door — 179 Piccadilly, London W1V 0BA — is the French Railways (SNCF — Société Nationale des Chemins de Fer Français) office, with its own up-to-date leaflets and information. There are special offers for railway tourists, available only to people who live outside France. I am not giving details of these: the SNCF office does that sort of thing better than anyone else. Air France offices are not far away: 158 New Bond Street, London W1Y 0AY.

After getting information from the French National Tourist Office and sending off its coupons to offices in the UK and in France for further information, another starting-point for collecting yet more information is ANIT, the recently formed Agence Nationale Pour l'Information Touristique, at 8 avenue de l'Opéra, 75001 Paris. To a large extent their work overlaps that of their London counterpart. But their magazine-like general brochure is useful; the 1985 one told me where to apply for full details of unusual holidays: learning to ride horses, to pilot hang-gliders and hot-air balloons, to weave baskets and make lace and clay pots; exploring underground caves, staying in *châteaux*, panning for gold in the Pyrenees,

23

tours on donkey-back, cheese-making, bread-baking; golf, master classes in violin playing, accompanied rambling on bike or on foot, mountaineering, courses for twelve enthusiasts on the care, maintenance and driving of a steam locomotive. . . . ANIT can be worth writing to, and calling on when in Paris.

Zooming to close-up distance, each region has its main tourist office (details from the FNTO or ANIT), and all towns and many villages have an Office du Tourisme (sometimes called a Syndicat d'Initiative) – addresses in the red Michelin guide (see page 66). The lower down one goes in the hierarchy of these French offices, the more important it is to enclose an International Reply Coupon, and not to expect a reply in English (though all of them will be able to understand a written enquiry in English). They all issue stacks of useful leaflets on accommodation and facilities, frequently updated.

As for architecture, scenery and 'natural curiosities', the Michelin 'green' guides cannot be called light bedside reading. But they are cheap, and on sale everywhere in France. They cover the country in nineteen booklets. Seven are available in English: Brittany, Châteaux of the Loire, Côte d'Azur, Normandy, Paris, Périgord, Provence. Succinct, impersonal, no-nonsense information about local history, geology and architecture; suggested excursions with clear directions; sketch maps and town plans. For my own taste, Michelin could pay more attention to visitable activities (making cheese, distilling brandy, auctioning fish) and save space by omitting some of the less remarkable features of ecclesiastical architecture. However, the local tourist office is usually good at providing information on establishments that welcome visitors. My collection of green guides leaves me unsatisfied, but I always have the relevant ones in the car, as a basic ration of hard facts.

Guides to hotels and restaurants are the subject of a separate chapter starting on page 60. But I cannot refrain from insisting that the current year's 'red' Michelin guide is almost essential. It appears in March and costs no more in Britain than in France, so one can spend many a long evening pipe-dreaming over it and mastering its complex system of symbols and abbreviations, as a preparation for a beautiful holiday.

People contemplating settling in France for long periods or for the rest of their lives will find Philip Holland's *Living in France Today* useful, if somewhat intimidating. It contains information on house purchase, income tax, insurance and French law.

Chapter 3

Maps and town plans

For navigating across France, any up-to-date small-scale map will do. Michelin covers the whole country on one 'red' map, no. 989, regularly revised. As this is too large for unfolding in the car or in a brisk breeze, it is more convenient to buy it in two halves: no. 998, the northern half, and no. 999, the southern half. The scale is 1cm to 10km.

As soon as one slows down, one needs the Michelin 'yellow' maps, at 1cm to 2km, or about 3 miles to the inch. More about these in the Motoring chapter, on page 31. It is sensible to wait until one is in France before buying yellow maps: they are on sale almost everywhere, they are cheaper than in Britain, and the turnover is so quick that there is less likelihood of getting an out-of-date one. (The year of publication is given in the top left corner, in tiny figures.)

The indispensable Michelin red guide, the subject of later pages, contains admirable town plans. These tie in with the yellow maps. When there is a red rectangle round a town on the yellow map, there is a town plan in the guide; the numbered exits on the plan are shown in the map.

The maps of the IGN (Institut Géographique National) are excellent, cartographically. Walkers find them useful, as they can be obtained in really large-scale versions, showing the *sentiers de grande randonnée* – long-distance ramblers' routes. But they are dearer, and do not have the advantage of tying in with the Michelin system.

Chapter 4

Stations Vertes

If one rents a *gîte* through the London Gîtes de France office
(see page 102 for chapter on *gîtes*), one gets a fair amount of
information about the facilities and attractions of the immediate area around each *gîte*. Other people who want a country
holiday, whether in a *gîte* secured by other means, or in a hotel
or in their own tent, can find a lot of useful information (in
French) in the annual *Stations Vertes* booklet. I am rather
chary of recommending too many guides, and perhaps when
motoring through France the red Michelin guide, one of the
other hotel-restaurant guides, maps, a small dictionary and the
collection of leaflets one started out with, plus those one
collects *en route* at Syndicats d'Initiative, are about enough.
(Well, I hope that if you've bought *this* book you will think it
worth a place somewhere in the car.) However, up-to-date
information, revised every year, and available free or nearly, is
worth having, and provides agreeable occupation, planning
and pondering during the long evenings at home. So I will put
in a word for the *Stations Vertes* guide.

Une station is not a railway station (though it is a Paris *métro* station) but a place where you stop. *Une station balnéaire* is a seaside resort, *une station verte* is in the country (*verte*: green). Some 500 villages and small towns scattered over France have decided to form an organisation that guarantees certain standards. Only if these are met can the place figure in the guide. There are of course hundreds of other villages that have not bothered to apply to join; for example, in the *département* I live in, the Hérault (a good region for holidays), I see only one village in the 1985 *Stations Vertes* book.

A village, town, etc., can attempt to get approval if it has:
attrait naturel – natural attractions (river for bathing and fishing, lake, woods, castles, other picturesque or interesting features);
hébergement – places to stay (hotels, campsites, self-catering accommodation);
équipement loisirs – leisure facilities (swimming pool or proper bathing place, sports field, tennis courts, etc.);
accueil – reception or welcome (Syndicat d'Initiative, permanent shops, official control of prices);
esthétique – 'aesthetic', meaning protection of natural sites, cleanliness and floral decorations in town and village.

Not all localities measure up to the standards, and some are on a waiting list while they pull their socks up. But I repeat that this is a voluntary affair, by no means covering all of France's agreeable country places.

To take an example of the information given in the 1985 edition: just two *stations vertes* were listed in the Ardèche region. Looking at one of these we find the number of inhabitants, the altitude, the roads it is on, the nearest railway station (from which there are three daily coach services); a good deal of *attrait* information (trout river, woods, footpaths with signposts, a big lake 13km away, lots of *châteaux* and ruins, etc.); fifty hotel rooms, one *gîte rural* and thirty-three *meublés*, which means self-catering places not officially classified as *gîtes ruraux*, fifty-five caravans for hire on farms, one 3-star campsite, two others, and camping on farms; a covered heated swimming pool, two tennis courts, horse riding, and clay-pigeon shooting. Address and phone number of the Syndicat d'Initiative. This is a typical entry.

Copies of the *Guide des Stations Vertes* can be obtained from La Fédération Française des Stations Vertes, Hôtel du Département de la Sarthe, 72040 LE MANS, France. Please enclose a couple of International Reply Coupons, obtainable from any British post office.

Chapter 5

Motoring

Crossing the water

Of course the car-ferry companies want us to book in advance. They get their money early, they can make forecasts of the traffic, and they can bully us into turning up with 45 minutes to spare, so that they can chivvy us around at their leisure. One must certainly book at peak times. But the last four crossings I made were in May, June, October and November. In each case I simply turned up at Calais or Dover, paid the single fare on the next boat or hovercraft leaving, and was on board in twenty minutes flat. This only works on the short sea route, where there is a boat every half hour or so. Perhaps one day I shall come a cropper and find that for some reason the boats are crowded and I have six hours to wait. I wouldn't mind that at Calais or Boulogne, but what can one do in Dover?

On board, the experienced Channel-crosser unpacks his picnic. The last touch of Britain is the passionate desire to form people into queues and make them wait. Not worth it for an instant coffee and a microwaved pseudo-hamburger. I get my 'duty-free', though, even going to France, thus saving a few centimes on cigarettes (including Gauloises) and about 20 per cent on gin and whisky. If camping or going to a *gîte*, whisky should be taken, for patriotic reasons: it impresses the natives and may be given to them in moderation. Do not buy cans of French or Belgian beer en route for France: it costs half the British price on the boat, but half the boat price on shore. (Going home, heroes buy their full duty-free beer allowance at the French port, 50 litres: a hundredweight. . . .)

Longer-distance night crossings are convenient if you live near the port, or if you have only a short holiday. Otherwise it should be remembered that a big comfortable room with bath in a French hotel costs less than a cabin.

Inebriated football supporters and tattooed hairy people in camping-cars that look as though there might be an additional petrol tank stuffed with drugs under the floor may have problems with French customs officers. Otherwise they are less trouble than British ones, some of whom seem occasionally aggrieved if they think you have had a good holiday and a smooth crossing. French customs officials are not exactly jovial, but they sometimes say *bon voyage*; otherwise they just look bored stiff and wave you through.

Having checked that you still have the car's log book, your driving licence (full), your green card, a red warning triangle (if the car has hazard warning lights, the triangle is optional; desirable, though, in case the car breaks down through electrical failure) and a set of spare bulbs, you are legally entitled to drive off, with seat belts secured and children under ten in back seats. You will of course have had your headlights adjusted in some way, for driving on the right. The French have yellow-tinted headlights; visitors don't *have* to. But I live in France, and like most Frenchmen when a set of white headlights zooms towards me I mutter 'Oafish foreigner!' and imagine I'm dazzled even when I'm not.

Only the rashly optimistic will have failed to take out extra insurance cover for car and people – the AA Five-Star policy for instance (available to non-members), which has the advantage that one can phone the AA centre at Boulogne free when in need of help. Insurance companies may have provided bilingual *constats à l'amiable* (European Accident Statement Forms) which, if filled in by both drivers agreeing on the facts, can simplify accident claims.

While we are waiting to emerge from the bowels of the boat, a moment's reflection. Statistics show that bronchitis and pneumonia are five times more frequent a cause of death in Britain than in France, so we can be reasonably optimistic about the weather. Statistics also show that France, with about the same population as the UK, has more cars but slightly fewer road accidents. Good again. But wait: in proportion to the number of cars, twice as many people are *killed* in road accidents in France. Why is this? For the same reason that there are more motor accidents in towns, but more people killed on open roads. It's the speed one hits things with that does the damage. So, in a way, it's good news: the UK is more like a big town, France is more like a large expanse of countryside. But in another way it's bad news. If we have an accident it is more likely to be a really nasty one than at home, especially if we insist on making faster averages than on Britain's more crowded roads. Let the French do the speeding. A high proportion of accidents to Britons occurs near the Channel ports, mainly in the homeward direction: belting along to catch the boat. Let it go. It is better to travel slowly than to arrive on a stretcher.

Driving on the right

If you have never driven on the right before, don't worry. It's easy. Having the steering-wheel on the 'wrong' side is fine for cautious driving. You are near the pavement and the cyclists, and you have a good view of the edge of the precipice. The actual overtaking of another vehicle is no problem either. Of course before deciding whether or not to overtake you have to edge out further, to get a good view: all the more reason to keep well behind preceding vehicles (better view) and to do less overtaking than at home. French lorries simply belt along, on main roads, so you won't lose much time if you let them overtake you instead.

Your passengers should never need to chorus 'Drive on the right!' every time you start moving, but train them to do so all the same, and tell them off if they forget. It might prevent an awkward moment after you have pulled over to the left of the road at a filling-station when there are no other cars zooming along to remind you, or after some other stop. They should also frequently remind you when you are trundling along a narrow road and (justifiably) are in the middle; there, you must be *mentally* on the right, or you will give a suddenly oncoming Frenchman an alarming problem if you pull sharply to the left. . . .

Britons are used to looking on the left for signs and signals that concern them, and of course the signs are on the right in France. Confusion can sometimes occur. If there are two lanes at traffic lights, one – say – for turning left and the other for going straight on or turning right, and you are in the right-hand lane and the two lights say different things, obviously it is the right-hand light, on the pavement, that you go by. On main roads there are signs in profusion, leaving no room for doubt. But in the remote district where I live there is a Y-junction. Driving up the Y one sees, bang in the middle between the two roads, a 'no entry' sign. This means that one takes the right-hand fork, otherwise one would have the 'no entry' sign on one's right as one went up the forbidden left-hand fork. But of course if the roads were more important there would be a 'no entry' sign on both sides of the left-hand fork.

If instead of driving your own car you are hiring one on the continent, it is useful to have a quiet practice run all by yourself. The change-over to driving on the right *and* being on the other side of the car and doing things with the right hand that one is used to doing with the left and vice versa (but keeping to the same old footwork) can take some getting used to. It is as well not to have to bother about going from A to B with the family until one has become acclimatised. I managed without mishap, but for six months when Sophie said 'Turn left' I quite often turned right, through over-compensation. Sophie herself had no trouble, though: she's a shifted sinistral – a left-hander brought up to use her right hand.

Priorité à droite

It is true that what with one thing and another (details later) *priorité à droite* – priority to the right – has been whittled away in recent years, but it is still the predominant system in France. It is the only rule of the road (apart from driving on the right) unknown in Britain; ignoring it causes accidents or embarrassment.

Britain is a small country with a lot of cars. When any road joins or crosses another road, it is clear who gives way to whom: if there are no traffic lights there are STOP or GIVE WAY signs, and the signs can be easily seen by the driver who doesn't have to give way.

Imagine France, years ago – a big country with few cars. No need for signs. They had a simple rule: give way to the driver coming from your right. At crossroads, right turns (the 'safe' turns – we are driving on the right) are easy; going straight on or turning left one may have to wait. Joining a straight road from a side road, if you're turning right you take precedence over a car coming from the left and going straight on, but if you're turning left and therefore crossing over the road you must wait for cars coming from the right. At a Y-junction the car coming down the 'eleven o'clock' road has priority over the car coming down the 'one o'clock' road. All very simple. Of course if four cars arrived at a crossroads simultaneously from the four points of the compass, they would all have to stay there for ever, but either they never do or common-sense takes over (*'Après vous, monsieur!' 'Mais non, monsieur, après vous!'* . . .). Anyway, that is the *priorité à droite* system. As long as one is aware of it, it causes no problems. Intersections where you have to give way to traffic coming from the right, without any road sign to remind you, will be found only where the sensible and law-abiding driver would be going fairly slowly; in towns, or on minor roads.

Priorité à droite does not apply, obviously, on motorways. The slip roads coming in from the right have 'give way' signs.

It does not apply on roads that are designated as *routes à caractère prioritaire,* which I shall call priority roads. You know you are on a priority road when you see the 'yellow square' sign:

The sign is repeated every three miles or so on the open road; often after junctions; and in the case of a priority road going through a built-up area, every kilometre at least. Traffic should give way to you, whether coming from left or right. This has led some British drivers to think (and some motoring correspondents to write) that *priorité à droite* has ceased to apply on all roads of any significance, except in built-up areas. Not so. Not only do you have priority on some of these roads in some built-up areas: you also lose your priority at an intersection in the open country when you see the yellow square with a bar sinister:

That means that at the intersection, *priorité à droite* will be the rule. (At such intersections there will often, but not always, be an additional reminder: ATTENTION, PRIORITÉ A DROITE.) After the intersection, if you are again on a priority road, you will see the plain yellow square again.

On entering a built-up area from a priority road, you will often lose priority status. This will always be clearly signalled with the 'bar sinister' sign; if you don't lose priority, there will be a plain yellow square to remind and reassure.

Roundabouts are a special case. I mean big roundabouts with a central reservation and special roundabout signs (arrows going round in a circle, often with the words VOUS N'AVEZ PAS LA PRIORITÉ below). These are of course navigated anti-clockwise (we are driving on the right) but in the accustomed British manner, give way to traffic already on the roundabout. Naturally the French made a great song and dance when this system came into action in mid-1984, and naturally the signs are big: it means abandoning *priorité à droite* habits and giving way to traffic coming from the left. Before mid-1984, *priorité à droite* applied: the determined driver shot straight on to the circuit, with cars already there giving way to him if he kept up his speed and didn't look at them. If hit, he was one up – *priorité à droite* means that battered right-hand wings are shameful, battered left-hand ones honourable. Then, when he had joined the dance, he had to stop to let other cars join in from the approach roads, which are of course on the right. This continued until the roundabout was choked with motionless cars, with more and more drivers on the approach roads trying to hoot their way into the fuming mass. It had worked well enough in the old days, when horseless carriages were rare; in more modern times, traffic lights had to be erected to prevent snarl-ups, and that defeated the aim of roundabouts.

However, if it's just a little roundabout, around a central lamp-post for example in a town or village, and there's no big roundabout sign but only an arrow showing which side of the lamp-post you go round, *priorité à droite* will still apply. You

can see why some French motorists get a little confused. . . .
Never mind, take it easy; if we hesitate we may be defrauded
of our theoretical priority, but we mustn't let little things like
that worry us.

If you are coming out from an earth road or a parking place,
you *never* have priority.

Speed

In the absence of signs showing something different, the
present (1986) limits are:

- on motorways 130km/h: about 80 m.p.h. But if wet,
  110km/h: about 68 m.p.h. ('Wet', here, means having the
  windscreen-wipers on.)
- on other dual-carriageway roads: 110km/h, about 68
  m.p.h. If wet, 100km/h, about 62 m.p.h.
- on ordinary roads: 90km/h, about 56 m.p.h. If wet,
  80km/h, about 50 m.p.h.
- in built-up areas: 60km/h, about 37 m.p.h. If wet, the same.

You enter a built-up area (*une agglomération*) when you meet
the sign showing the name of the town or village, in black or
dark blue capital letters on a white background; the more
modern signs have a red border round them. No further
indication is needed; when you meet that sign you are in a
60km/h area. There may be '60' reminder signs (they have
rappel below them) here and there. Of course there might be a
different speed limit. In that case it will be clearly shown.

You leave the *agglomération* when you meet the same sign
'crossed out' with a diagonal red stripe. There is no need for a
de-restriction sign – you are out.

A sign giving the name of a village in white lower-case
letters on a dark blue background just tells us the name of the
little place. It isn't an *agglomération*, only a *lieu-dit:* no 60km/h
limit (though of course there might be a speed limit indicated
in the normal way).

The police have radar and other devices. If caught speeding, a driver may get away with a surprisingly heavy on-the-spot fine and a breathalyser test. Many French drivers are under the impression that they can legally exceed the speed limit by 10 per cent, and then they do a further 10 per cent to show their virility, so do not be puzzled if you are overtaken when doing the maximum. It will often happen, and sometimes you will see the driver later on, as he blows into the bag. If two policemen on big motorbikes, bristling with firearms, overtake you and wave you down, it is advisable to come to a dignified halt. (They *aim* at the tyres. . . .)

If an oncoming driver flashes his headlights at you, the most probable meaning is 'I am a delinquent and I expect you are too, so watch it, the cops are round the corner.' Otherwise it might mean some other hazard on the road, or just 'Get out of my way.' It almost never means 'After you.'

The above remarks, and some later ones, may seem alarming and discouraging. That is only because I take driving rather seriously, like mountaineering or big-game hunting. Driving in France has more moments of pleasure than in England. In 180,000 miles of French driving I have had no accidents but one near miss; and the police have stopped me once, to see if I was wearing my seat belt (I was). Incidentally, I have never had anything stolen from my car in France, but I'm careful about that. My British record is almost the same, except that my seat belt was never checked. (I had a suitcase stolen from my car in Plymouth in 1961.) Perhaps I have been lucky, so far.

Motorways

Autoroutes are motorways, and have numbers preceded by the letter A. The driving technique is essentially the same as in Britain.

You pay to use an autoroute. When you arrive at a *péage* (toll-booth) there are three possibilities:
1) You press a knob marked POUSSEZ and a ticket (conveniently called *un ticket*) pops out. Keep it carefully: it

shows where you joined the autoroute. When you leave the autoroute you will have to produce it, and pay.

2) A person asks for some money. No language problem, usually, as an electronic machine shows the sum due. This will of course be the drill if you have previously taken a ticket.

3) If you have been on a stretch with a smallish fixed charge, there may be an automatic machine. A kilometre or two beforehand you will have seen a sign: PRÉPAREZ VOTRE MONNAIE – prepare your change, or rather, get your passenger to prepare it. A sign shows how much to pay, and which coins are accepted. You throw them into a basket, the machine counts them and you get the green light. At all such *péages* there are manned booths for people without the right change.

Of course the attendants, knobs and baskets are on the wrong side if you have a British car.

You may stop on the verge (*la bande d'arrêt d'urgence*) in emergency only. If you need help, there is a telephone roughly every 2 kilometres (1¼ miles). This puts you in touch, free, with the Centre de Sécurité, who will send (not free) a repair truck (*un dépanneur*) or first aid (*le service de secours*). 'I have run out of petrol' is *J'ai une panne sèche* (a dry breakdown). You may walk along the verge; little arrows show the direction of the nearest phone. Trying to hitch a lift is forbidden.

There are *aires de repos*, sometimes with pleasant views, for parking, with lavatories and running water, usually drinkable (if not, it will be labelled EAU NON POTABLE), and quite often a picnic area with tables and benches – and rubbish bins.

And there are *aires de services*: service stations, usually with a café and sometimes with a restaurant (occasionally quite good for grills, notably the *Quatre Pentes* chain).

Some of these *aires* have tourist information offices, with currency exchange, hotel reservation facilities and camping information.

Folders in several languages giving motorway maps with details of the various *aires* can sometimes be obtained from a *péage* and usually at *aires de services*. Very useful for planning stops. Try the Piccadilly Tourist Office.

The signs on the motorway are mostly international. When approaching a tunnel, ALLUMEZ VOS FEUX or ALLUMEZ VOS PHARES means put on your dipped headlights. ÉTEIGNEZ VOS FEUX means switch them off.

In the uphill direction there is often an extra lane for slow vehicles. The sign is VÉHICULES LENTS, sometimes with an arrow, sometimes with the instruction SERREZ A DROITE (keep well over to the right, take the right-hand lane). 'Slow' means below 60km/h, about 37 m.p.h.

Autoroutes, in other words, present no problems unknown to the British motorway user, except finding the cash. They are a quick, dull way of covering the ground. The Britons who come to grief on them are often those who insist on doing another 100 or 200 miles when they need a rest or a night's sleep.

The service station – la station-service

You do not want *pétrole*. That is the crude oil that goes slurp slurp into the OPEC barrels (it means paraffin, too – don't put petrol into *une lampe à pétrole*!).

Petrol is *essence* (f.). It comes in two grades; the lower grade is normally referred to as *essence* and the higher as *super*. Diesel fuel is *gas-oil* (m.), sometimes called *gazole*.

'100 francs' worth of super, please' – *Pour cent francs de super, s'il vous plaît*
'Fill her up' – *Faites le plein*
'Check the oil' – *Vérifiez l'huile*
'Check the tyres' – *Vérifiez les pneus* (the *p* is pronounced; the word rhymes with 'fur')

All such instructions should include *s'il vous plaît* and *monsieur, madame* or *mademoiselle*. The French are more verbally polite than the British. They may wish you *bonne route* or *bonne continuation* or *bon retour*, the correct response being *merci, et au revoir*.

Of course there will be less of such human contact at a busy *station-service* on the autoroute than when you stop at a two-pump place in a one-horse village. There, a five-minute chat will be appreciated, about where you come from, where you are going, and the chap's second cousin who spent a week in Bootle twenty years ago when she was at school.

Instead of doing conversions from pounds per square inch into kilograms per square centimetre, bring your own tyre gauge.

Trouble in the works – le garage

The red Michelin guide shows, for each town, which garages are agents for which makes of car. Two-thirds of current new cars registered are French models, and the more popular German and Italian cars make up the rest. British-made cars, alas, are few and far between; so are their agents. If you take a British-made car to France it would be sensible to have the safeguard of the AA's or the RAC's schemes whereby spare parts can be flown out and arrangements made in case your car has to be left behind. But France is lavishly covered with Renault, Citroën and Peugeot agents, and there is a good sprinkling of Volkswagen, Mercedes and Fiat places.

I make no apology for repeating that the French are at their best when they are their own bosses, or – failing that – when they are given enough responsibility to avoid feeling mere cogs in a machine; and that human relationships, even momentary ones, can rival the cash nexus. For a straightforward routine job, including major replacements, a big specialist garage is the most efficient solution. But for anything odd, especially near closing time, do not despise the one-man-and-a-boy garage. The man may regard a minor fault on an exotic car as a challenge to his skill and ingenuity. Even if your car is not exotic, you are; at a big garage a reasonable excuse might be found to give you the brush-off, but the small independent man is likely to go beyond the call of duty, doing a favour of his own free will and taking a lot of trouble. In return, you have brightened his day, he has made an interesting human contact and shown what a kind, resourceful chap he is. He will have something to talk about at supper. I don't say they're all like that, but it's surprising how many are.

A great deal can be done without language; the sight and sound of the offending mechanism are eloquent. Beyond that, the most useful technical word in the everyday vocabulary of spoken French (rarely taught in British schools; it is non-U) is *le machin*, meaning the whatsit or the thingummy. It is pronounced, roughly, le mash-ANG; and not to be confused with the standard French *la machine*, which is pronounced la mash-EEN and means the machine. *Ce machin-là* – that thingummy there. Don't waste time with a technical dictionary if you can point to the object. There is also *le truc*: another word for a thingummy; it can also mean a dodge, trick or cunning wheeze. (These two valuable words are not to be used on formal or literary occasions; almost everybody uses them on almost all other occasions but feels a bit guilty unless he's a garage mechanic; that's education.) If the mechanic can't fix the *machin* that has gone wrong in your car, he may be able to improvise a *truc* to help you on your way.

'I've broken down' – *Je suis en panne*
a noise – *un bruit*
a squeak – *un grincement*
some smoke – *de la fumée*
'the —— doesn't work' – *le —— ne marche pas*
'the —— is making a funny noise' – *le —— fait un bruit anormal*
'there's a smell of burning' – *cela sent le brûlé*
'the —— is broken' – *le —— est cassé* (— *est foutu* is slang, but often employed in this context to mean broken or beyond repair or worn out)
'it's overheating' – *cela surchauffe*
an oil leak – *une fuite d'huile*
a petrol leak – *une fuite d'essence*

a water leak – *une fuite d'eau*

a brake fluid leak – *une fuite de liquide de freins* (but *Lockheed* is often loosely used instead of *liquide de freins*)

a spare part – *une pièce détachée*

to do an oil change – *vidanger* (strictly, this means to empty the old oil, but is generally used for the complete operation)

'will it take long?' – *ce sera vite fait?*

Bits and pieces

air filter – *le filtre à air*

axle – *l'essieu* (m.)

battery – *la batterie*

big end – *la bielle* (strictly, the connecting-rod)

brake – *le frein*

carburettor – *le carburateur*

choke – *le starter* (NB see 'starter' below)

clutch – *l'embrayage* (m.)

contact breaker – *le rupteur*

cooling fan – *le ventilateur*

crankshaft bearing – *le palier*

distributor – *l'allumeur*

engine – *le moteur*

exhaust pipe – *le tuyau d'échappement*

fan belt (or other transmission belt) – *le courroie* (but a seat belt is *une ceinture de sécurité*)

fuse – *le fusible*

gear box – *la boîte de vitesses*

    first, second, third, top gear – *première, deuxième, troisième, quatrième vitesse;* reverse – *marche arrière;* neutral – *le point mort*

ignition – *l'allumage* (m.)

indicator – *le (feu) clignotant*

light bulb – *une ampoule*

oil – *l'huile*

puncture (tyre) – *le pneu crevé*

silencer – *le silencieux*
spare part – *une pièce détachée*
spark plug – *la bougie*
starter – *le démarreur* (NB see 'choke' above)
steering system – *la direction*
suspension – *la suspension*
tappet – *le culbuteur*
tyre – *le pneu* (the 'p' is pronounced; it rhymes with 'fur')
valve (engine) – *la soupape*
wheel – *la roue* (but the steering-wheel is *le volant*)
windscreen – *le pare-brise*
windscreen-wiper – *l'essuie-glace* (m.)

A Mini, a Ford, etc., are *une* Mini, *une* Ford – feminine, because they are short for *une voiture Mini, Ford,* etc.

Signs and symbols

Traffic lights (*feux tricolores*, or 'three-coloured fires') are the same as in Britain, except that they go straight from red to green. A calculation of when the change is likely to occur can be attempted by watching the other lights or the pedestrian lights, if one is keen on making a dramatic start.

Filter lights are amber or sometimes green, and usually flashing. Traffic on other roads has priority.

Flashing amber lights mean proceed with caution, observing the appropriate priority rules.

At some level crossings, near aerodromes, before swing bridges and near fire-brigade stations there may be a single flashing red light. This means stop.

'P', as in Britain, indicates a car park. In small towns this will often be free, and unlimited. For street parking, it may be STATIONNEMENT ALTERNÉ SEMI-MENSUEL: on one side of the street (often the side with odd-numbered houses) until the evening (between 8.30 and 9 p.m., to be precise) of the 15th, and the other side until the end of the month.

In a *zone bleu* you get free parking for 1½ hours in the daytime, but with a proper French lunch-hour parking time (11.30 a.m. − 2.30 p.m.). You must have *un disque de stationnement*. This is a cardboard thing, obtainable from the tobacconist: you shift the disc to show the time you arrived and the time you have to go, and leave it to be seen through the windscreen. Unlimited night parking.

If you have to pay, there are parking meters, as at home. If below the 'P' sign there is the word HORODATEUR, you must find a *horodateur* somewhere in the parking area. It is a slot machine. You put in your money, and a ticket pops out. Leave it so that it can be seen by *le contractuel* (the meter-person) through your windscreen.

The 'yellow square' and the roundabout sign have been dealt with under the section *Priorité à droite*. Other signs are international, as in Britain, or easily understood − there is a nice one near where I live showing a wild boar, such animals being jay-walkers.

Some signs are in words, often under a 'danger' sign. Here is a collection − incomplete, since although some are standard others may be thought up by local councils.

absence de marquage − no white lines on road (newly surfaced)

accôtements . . . followed by any one of a number of adjectives (*instables, meubles, non consolides* . . .) − soft shoulder, verge unsafe. (There is a French word *verge* but it does not mean an *accôtement*; an English lady of my acquaintance startled a French driver and passenger by saying '*Attention aux verges!*' It means a penis. In Britain the sign 'Soft Verges' causes mixed reactions among French visitors.)

arbres inclinés − trees leaning over; don't worry unless you're driving a double-decker bus.

arret autocars − bus stop

arrosage − watering of crops by spray; you may need the wipers.

ball-trap – not to worry. Not an official road-sign. It shows the way to the place where you can indulge in clay-pigeon shooting.

betteraves – not jay-walking beetroots, but mud and sugar-beet on the road, in northern parts.

boue – mud

cédez le passage – give way (usually an addition to the international 'give way' sign)

centre ville – town centre

chantier mobile – an alternative to 'travaux', road work in progress. Nothing to do with *chanter*, to sing; *un chantier* is a place, usually in the open, where some kind of work (building houses, boats, roads . . .) is going on. At the other end you may see *fin de chantier* – the end of the road-works.

chaussée déformée – bumpy road surface

chute de pierres – accompanied by a dramatic sign showing a massive boulder crashing off a mountain; it means that stones may get on the road, not that one is in danger of being squashed flat.

créneau de dépassement à X km – overtaking possible in X km

deux roues (2 roues) – bicycles and motor-bicycles

déviation – diversion (usually a yellow signpost)

éboulement – landslide; or a lot of mud, etc., on road

élagage – tree lopping in progress

gravillons – loose chippings, gravel. The French are generous with these. After a couple of months most of them have shifted to the side of the road, together with fragments of windscreen. It is safer to go slow and get bombarded by overtaking cars: an airborne *gravillon* has negligible speed – it's the speed at which you hit the one thrown up by cars coming in the opposite direction that can do the damage. At the end of a stretch of this sort of thing, garages advertise *pose de pare-brise* – windscreens fitted. Actually I have lost only one windscreen in many miles of motoring in France, but I am not an exciting driver.

interdit par submersion – no thoroughfare when under water

piste cyclable – cycle path

poids lourds – literally, 'heavyweights'; big lorries. This often indicates the street or road they should take, but not you. Or a special speed limit for them – sometimes *marchez au pas*, walking speed, on some bridges.

rainurage – sometimes seen on motorways and other main roads, the sign concerns *deux roues:* longitudinal grooves which can be awkward for motor-bicycles.

rappel – reminder. Under a repeated sign.

rocade – expressway in town (confusion can arise when Britons think *rocade* is the name of a town they don't want to go to, as in the sign PARIS PAR ROCADE).

route barrée – road closed

sortie de camions (or *sortie d'usine, de carrière*) – lorries may emerge, from a factory or a quarry.

toutes directions – literally 'all directions', but there is often another sign pointing in the direction of *centre ville*, so this sign means 'through traffic'. In some towns, out of the rush hour, it may be quicker and more interesting to ignore the sign and go straight through the town instead of going all the way round via dull modern suburbs, but if you don't know the town it is sensible to go *toutes directions* and look out for later signposts.

travaux – road works

un seul camion sur le pont – only one lorry at a time on the bridge

véhicules surbaissés attention! – low-slung cars, take care; you may lose your exhaust-pipe at a dip in the road surface.

verglas – risk of ice on road

voie unique – one carriageway (at narrow bridge, etc., usually accompanied by a sign showing who has the priority; if you want to go in the direction of the red arrow, wait for the car facing you).

Alternative Routes and Bison Futé

An *itinéraire bis* is an alternative route for avoiding crowded roads at peak holiday periods. But first, a word about *Bison Futé*, or Wily Buffalo. The French Ministry of Transport dreamed him up years ago. He used to play his tom-tom on the radio, and in a Red Indian sort of voice announced when and where the pale-faces were likely to be on the warpath, and how to avoid them. Then they issued a map, revised annually, called La Carte de Bison Futé, which showed these alternative routes; and they were signposted. Nowadays the Red Indian gimmick seems to have evaporated (protests about racism?) but not the name; La Carte de Bison Futé is still issued – and very useful it is too. It is free, either from the French National Tourist Office in Piccadilly or from tourist information offices as soon as you get to France. Currently it is a booklet, with a fair amount of useful information in it as well as the map. The map, though not of Michelin quality, is useful in itself, because the signs tend to show an ultimate destination – Paris, for example – which may be 400 miles away, whereas one wants generally to know what intermediate places an *itinéraire bis* goes through.

Itinéraire bis signs are either green, with white lettering, or yellow with black lettering and the word *bis* in a circle. The yellow ones are replacing the green ones, but at the time of writing there are still plenty of green ones about. (*Bis*, in this context, means secondary; but there is a touch of *bison* about it; the French are only too fond of puns.)

Sometimes the roads recommended are unsuitable for caravans. In that case a crossed-out caravan symbol is shown at the beginning of the route. The routes are of course slower, in normal circumstances, than the main roads. They are often pleasanter. One can be even more *futé* than the *Bison* himself, by using the yellow large-scale Michelin maps and avoiding the minor roads that the main-road avoiders are using. Another good reason for getting a *Bison Futé* map.

Much shorter alternative routes, called *itinéraires de délestage*, have yellow signs (without *bis* on them). These are for making a detour round notorious bottle-necks at peak moments.

Drinking and driving

The French police naturally breathalyse any driver who is involved in any sort of accident or infringes the regulations in any way. They also make random tests. The limit is the same as in Britain. If one is over the limit but has done nothing else wrong, one might get away with a hefty on-the-spot fine and the immobilisation of one's car for a few hours.

The French Highway Code gives the limit as 0.8 gram of alcohol per litre. It says that a half bottle of wine, drunk with a meal by a man of 75kg (about 11½ stones) will produce an alcohol level of 0.5 gram, which is thought to be just about reasonable (a half litre of normal French beer produces 0.19). But on an empty stomach the figure would rise to 0.74 gram – dangerously near the limit. What the French mean by a meal is something more than a quick sandwich, however. . . . I just can't win, because if I have a proper French meal and a half bottle of wine with it, I tend to drop off to sleep on a warm afternoon, and if I crash my car and my 11½ snoozing stones into something it will be a poor consolation to be able to prove that I'm well below the limit.

Route planning, zooming and pottering

France is a lovely land for motoring in, especially for those who like to take it easy. Wide open spaces, forests, valleys . . . a network of well-maintained secondary roads with villages and country towns conveniently scattered over an area two and a half times bigger than Great Britain (four times the size of England). One recent Easter Monday the radio was predicting crowded roads and traffic jams, and I'm sure it was right as far as the main arteries were concerned. But we took the minor roads to go from Montpellier to Bergerac, about 200 miles through woods and along streams and rivers; five hours' actual driving and we hardly saw another car. We had two delays. One was The Giant Omelette, which was being made as the high spot of a village fair (I forget the diameter, but it was considerable); the other was a flock of sheep and goats, tinkling their bells, which we had to follow for five minutes. We took eight hours on the journey, though. The non-driving time was spent picnicking and in stopping and staring whenever we felt like it, which was often. Over a delicious dinner at the hotel at Bergerac we agreed that it had been a well-spent Bank Holiday Monday.

On the other hand, there is the motorway. Bombing down the 600 miles from Calais to Avignon, or the 750 miles to Nice or Perpignan, is feasible all in one go with a relief driver, and even single handed with stops every two hours for black coffee and deep breathing exercises, but I would do almost anything to avoid starting and finishing a holiday like that. I mean, you can't call a motorway *France*. . . . Civilised roads have avenues of poplars or plane trees, cheap or elegant restaurants with tables under the wisteria, cafés with a view of the river and parasols advertising Pernod; but the only real difference between the M1 and the *Autoroute du Soleil* (the Motorway of the Sun), in high summer, is that there's too darn much *soleil* and it's difficult to park in the shade. Over 100°F in the car is no fun. The motorway cafés are a bit different, but when you've seen one you've seen the lot. And you're spending money on motorway tolls that could pay for a decent double room in an interesting place, if you took an extra night.

Some unfortunate people have short holidays; they can put the car on the train at Boulogne in the evening and wake up at Avignon next morning. All they need is the money. The fare sounds steep, but less steep when one sets off against it the night's bed, the tolls, the petrol, and the wear and tear on driver, passengers and car; a bonus of two days' extra holiday, one at each end. (Long-distance motorway driving isn't a holiday, it's work.)

Having worked that out, and having winced at the exorbitant fare a car has to pay to cross the Channel in the high season, the next step is to consider leaving the thing in the garage, going by train and boat or by air, and hiring a car at the other end – just for pottering. It can make sense to hire a car for only part of one's holiday, too. There are fly-drive arrangements, and Hertz, Avis, Europcar and other firms have offices in both countries and can give the current rates.

Personally (*moi, personellement, je,* as they say), if I had three weeks' holiday and wanted to spend it in a *gîte* in the south, I would book the *gîte* for a fortnight and spend 3½ days getting there and 3½ days getting back, by a different route. And I would use secondary roads, the yellow or white ones on the large-scale Michelin maps. And I wouldn't let anyone, not even Arthur Eperon, tell me which way to go; I would zig-zag around. And if one day, what with poking my nose here and there and buying my picnic, I didn't get away until eleven in the morning, and at three o'clock I found a delightful little town or village with a charming little hotel offering an interesting dinner menu at bargain rates, I'd say, like the great Macmahon: *j'y suis, j'y reste*: blowed if I move. I might never find that perfect place again. . . . Happiness – *luxe, calme et volupté* – is having a wife like Sophie and no boat to catch.

Zoom or potter, one needs to know in which direction to go. For grand strategy, any small-scale map showing the whole of France will do. Michelin does one, but there are plenty of others. It is when one comes down nearer the surface that Michelin scores.

The Michelin yellow maps are large-scale (1cm to 2km, or about 3 miles to the inch), and it would be overdoing it to buy a lot of them before starting out. But they are very cheap, at least in France, and they can be bought everywhere: at motorway cafés and in every newspaper shop in every village. It is quite practicable to pick them up as and when the need arises. They give a lot of information about even very minor roads, and there is Michelin's subjective but fairly reliable assessment of viewpoints and picturesque roads (Michelin is fonder of forest scenery than open rolling countryside). Of course one has the red Michelin guide: numbered town exits on the yellow maps are repeated on the town plans in the guide, and every place mentioned in the red guide has its name underlined in red on the yellow map.

Motorways are motorways. Main roads can be nice or rather nasty; secondary roads, yellow on the Michelin maps, can be as quick as main roads, or quicker if you plan a route that avoids big towns without bypasses. As soon as I am off the motorway I use a yellow map, and I don't hesitate to buy one even if I'm going to use it only for an hour. Reliable information can be beyond price, and these maps cost about as much as a couple of newspapers. It is amazing how mean some people are about information. How much is a delightful afternoon, instead of a dull one, worth?

A useful technique, if one has a fair amount of ground to cover in a limited time, is to alternate two-hour stretches on the motorway with two-hour stretches on lesser roads, using the yellow maps for the latter, and taking meal-breaks and doing a little shopping in likely towns or villages.

Pedestrian crossings

French pedestrian crossings have stripes but not beacons. Motorists should treat them as British zebras. Pedestrians, on the other hand, should not. They should be regarded as attempts to show where a prudent walker might perhaps cross with his wits about him.

French visitors to Britain are loud in their praises of our drivers' zebra drill. The difference is no doubt partly due to superior virtue. But to be fair, there is the fact that British zebras are established only where research shows that they will be constantly used; when a driver sees a beacon he knows he will probably have to stop. The French paint stripes much more lavishly. Every day I drive through a tiny French village where there are three zebras for fifty inhabitants; not once a month do I have to stop. There is some excuse when French drivers do not approach every zebra cautiously.

But squashing pedestrians on zebras is viewed as seriously in France as in Britain.

Chapter 6

Trains

The French Railways (Société National des Chemins de Fer Français – SNCF) office, 179 Piccadilly, London, W1V 0BA, is the place for up-to-date details of services, including special offers for the young, the old, and even those in-between. For example, in 1985 there was the *France Vacances Spécial* rail rover ticket, available only if you lived outside France. For £94, or £137 first class, you got a travel credit of eight days, which could be taken one by one over a period of one month, plus bonuses such as free travel by bus and metro in Paris, and reduced rate car hire at over 200 railway stations. No doubt this will continue – a bargain for people who want to criss-cross the country, staying put for three or four days here and there.

If you have booked your rail journey in Britain, you will have no problems with *le compostage* and *TGV* (*train de grande vitesse* – high speed train) reservation; it has all been done for you. What follows is mainly for people buying their tickets in France.

Le compostage is IMPORTANT. You can buy your ticket at any time, up to two months in advance. But before you get on your train you must *composter* it yourself – date-stamp it. You stick it in a date-stamping machine (COMPOSTEZ VOTRE BILLET) at the entrance to the platforms (*les quais*). If you fail to do this you have not got a valid ticket; when the inspector comes round (as he certainly will) you will have to pay a fine. This is fair enough: if you didn't compost it, you could travel on that line for two months, up and down every day, were it not for the stern inspector. Now what happens if you rush to the station, compost your ticket, and miss your train? If there's another one that day, your composted ticket is valid for it; but if there isn't, then you will have to get your ticket uncom- posted. Go to the ticket office beating your breast and say, *Hélas, monsieur, j'ai raté mon train* – and the kind man will restore the virginity of the document.

Seats can be reserved on most trains when buying tickets (*fumeurs, non-fumeurs, coin-fenêtre, coin-couloir:* smokers, non- smokers, corner seat by the window, corner seat by the corridor or aisle). They *must* be reserved if you are going by the *TGV*. If for some reason you have your ticket but have not reserved your seat on the *TGV*, there is an electronic machine at the station that will do the job any time from an hour and a half before the time of departure; even in the last few moments (but you do not get a choice of *fumeurs, non-fumeurs*, etc.).

On some trains, including the *TGV* on certain days and times, an extra charge is payable. If you are booking from Britain, this should have been taken care of. If you are buying your ticket and reserving your seat in France, the *supplément* will of course be included. Otherwise, it is better to enquire about *le supplément* at the station and pay it there – it costs more on the train.

The trains and services of the SNCF seem generally to be thought superior to those of British Railways. But there are criticisms of the food and drink available on board, especially of their price. Taking a picnic is to be recommended (no hardship in France – see page 95) and above all some little bottles, not forgetting something to open them with. Going first class is even more delightful when one spreads a gourmet picnic around.

For those in a hurry there are night trains with basic *couchettes* (six bodies, mixed sexes, per second-class compartment; four in the first-class) and more comfortable sleepers (*voitures-lits*). Travellers with more leisure should remember that a hotel room for the night usually costs less than a berth on the train.

La carte couple is obtainable while you wait at major stations. With this, one member of the couple pays full fare and the other member goes half-price when they are travelling together at off-peak times. This *carte* cannot be obtained in Britain, but British married couples have got theirs in France by producing passports to show their married status. So have some unmarried ones, by producing evidence that they share an address, but it depends on the official on duty (unmarried French couples can produce a *certificat de concubinage*). Passport-sized photographs are needed.

Bicycles can be hired, by the day or longer, at over 250 stations. Up-to-date details from the SNCF office, and of course French stations.

Chapter 7

Paris

Paris is the most beautiful city in the world. Paris is hell, because of the motorcars. And so on. Paris can be *done*, painstakingly, with a good guide book (there are many; the English-language Michelin green guide, scrupulously followed, ensures that not a sight goes unseen); and Paris can be savoured by idling at random, stopping and staring ... This is a book about France in general, not about Paris in particular. One or two points are worth making:

- Driving in Paris is delightful from dawn to breakfast time on a Sunday morning in high summer. It is no fun at all at any other time. Here is the technique for anyone who is touring France by car and wants to pass two or three days in Paris: spend a night in a pleasant town outside Paris that is on a main railway line (Fontainebleau?), having chosen a hotel with a garage. Leave the car there; the garage fee plus the rail fare is a bargain compared with the pain and anguish of being lumbered with a car in central Paris. Go in by rail in the morning. At the mainline station (Gare d'Austerlitz, de l'Est, de Lyon, du Nord) and at the air terminal (Gare des Invalides) there are tourist offices, where multi-lingual *Hôtesses de France* are waiting to pick up the phone on your behalf and find you a room in a hotel in the price category (one, two, three or four stars) of your choice, at a very small charge for this service (it depends on the category of hotel). Pick up a sheaf of up-to-date tourist leaflets, and depart by taxi, tranquilly, for your hotel. Two or three days later, return to your car, spend the night, and drive off into the countryside at peace with the world. (Sophie and I, living in France, sometimes do likewise when visiting London; we leave the car at a hotel in Calais . . .)

- The Office de Tourisme de Paris is at 127 avenue des Champs-Elysées, 75008 Paris. It provides masses of leaflets in English and in French, giving details of what's on (events, exhibitions, markets, theatres, sight-seeing, etc.). They will find hotel rooms in Paris, and in at least one chain's hotels in the provinces. Short-stay furnished flat-hunting can start here. The office is open every day including Sundays, until 10 p.m. in the summer and 8 p.m. in the winter.

- The *métro* (underground) is easy. There are big maps of Paris, and of the *métro* lines, at street level at every station. The lines are known by the stations at their ends, so one follows signs saying DIRECTION SO-AND-SO, according to the station at the end of that line. Intersections for changing trains are *correspondances*. The *métro* has a flat-rate system: one journey, one ticket. It is cheaper, and saves time, to buy a *carnet* of ten tickets, which can also be used on buses. Or one can buy a two-day, four-day or seven-day *Billet de Tourisme* – unlimited bus and metro travel.

- Sight-seeing coach tours? Bus route 24 is much cheaper. The RATP (Régie Autonome des Transports Parisiens – Paris Transport Authority) issues leaflets showing bus routes and recommends several as interesting rides.

- Many people swear by the *Plan de Paris*, published by Leconte. There are cheaper town plans, and free ones, but

Leconte gives a lot of useful information for people making a prolonged stay.

- Avoiding Paris by car: if using motorways it may be quicker to go to Paris, and zoom round the *boulevard périphérique* (remembering that Boulogne, on a signpost, does not mean the Channel port but a Paris district) but it cannot be called a pleasure. A Michelin map, no. 196, *Environs de Paris*, covers a rectangle 80 miles by 60 at 1cm–1km, twice the yellow map scale, allowing one to pick a leisurely way round instead. But there is much to be said for giving Paris an even wider berth – secondary roads through Normandy can lead one through delightful places, and on the other side the champagne region (via Laon, Épernay, etc.) has its charm.

Chapter 8

Hotels and restaurants

Sophie and I know lots of cheerful clean hotels where, for half the British price, we get a comfortable room with private bath and loo, and a balcony looking on to a pleasant river with smiling cows on its banks, a snow-capped mountain, a lake surrounded by vineyards, a cathedral, the sort of village square that gets its photograph in coffee-table books . . . not all seen from the same balcony, but dotted here and there throughout France. And as for restaurants: whenever we meet another pair of food-and-drink bores the swapping of *bonnes petites adresses* goes on until midnight.

I am not naming them here. I want this book to be useful for as long as possible. They say that fishing tackle is a better present for a hungry man living near the sea than a dozen tins of sardines. The fishing tackle in this book consists of general advice, together with the recommendation to use at least the current year's Michelin hotel and restaurant guide. If I were given £100,000 and the loan of a team of investigators for a year I could not be as comprehensive as Michelin. I hope that French traditions, habits and standards will remain gratifyingly stable, but chefs move on and individual establishments improve or deteriorate. It is illuminating to compare one year's Michelin with the next. . . .

And then I am grateful to you for reading this book, and I hope that many more intelligent, enterprising people will follow your example. If they do, what might happen if I revealed my little handful of good addresses? Talking of favourite taverns in Athens, Patrick Leigh Fermor says: 'Docile flocks converge . . . The Athenians who ate there for generations have long since fled . . . The works of writers mentioning these places by name should be publicly burnt by the common hangman.'*

I wouldn't want to see the works of, say, Arthur Eperon burnt. His *Travellers' France, Le Weekend* and *French Selection,* for example, give an excellent notion of what typical French hotels and restaurants are like. Having read his books with pleasure, one knows the kind of thing to expect. I am sure that Mr Eperon and other successful writers of that sort of book would be the first to admit that they have not sampled more than a fraction of France's hotels and restaurants, and that their readers have a fair chance of finding places as good as theirs if they just follow their noses. Experienced Francophiles, reading *Travellers' France* (which brilliantly puts the case for taking secondary roads and pottering slowly; and then suggests some routes), will mutter 'Well I might try that some time, but why didn't he go *this* way? And stay *there*? And eat *that*?' France is a big rich land, full of treasures. . . .

It does no harm to recommend the Ritz. Smaller places can be vulnerable. There was a good article by Paul Levy in the *Observer* in January 1985. He tells of the meal he had most enjoyed in the previous six months. It wasn't the one at L'Archestrate or the one at Taillevent (both in Paris; cost a bomb) or even the one at the Dorchester, where 'Anton Mosimann, the best chef in England, fed nine of the best chefs in Europe.' No, it was at a tiny village in the Ardèche, just

* Patrick Leigh Fermor, *Roumeli,* Penguin Books, 1983

south of Lyon. He describes it lovingly. ... It cost 40 francs a head – about £3.50 at that time. Also eating were the *patronne*, her two sisters-in-law, their husbands and children, five paying guests and the man who was repairing the church. Mr Levy has his heart in the right place, but he goes on to *give the address*. If a mere five thousand of the *Observer*'s readers turned up there in 1985, this may have happened: (1) Mr Levy and his fellow eaters got *saucisson* from the *patronne's* own pig, but the 1985 *saucissons* came from a wholesaler; (2) one day, as happens with all of us, something went wrong in the kitchen, but the Britons were still so happy (French food when somewhat under par being jolly good by British standards, especially when the wine flows freely) that the *patronne* learnt that corners could be safely cut; (3) the chap who was repairing the church said 'This place is only for tourists – I'm off to the other place round the corner.'; and (4) the 'two marvellous ladies' who ran it made a lot of money; being only human they sold out for a good round sum on the strength of their turnover account. The new owners put plastic beams on the ceiling, stopped raising chickens and growing tarragon and laid in a deep-freeze full of *magret de canard*.

Let us hope it didn't happen. Fortunately there are places like the one Mr Levy found in a surprisingly large number of villages. Although relying on Michelin is usually safe, villages off the beaten track do not figure in it unless there is something exceptional about the local hotel or restaurant. The presence of cheerful locals enjoying their food is a good sign. A British-registered car parked outside should not put one off, however: many of our compatriots love *la vraie cuisine française*, and are more French than the French at winkling out *une bonne petite adresse*. But it is sad when a good place becomes a rip-off GB-plate ghetto because of a well-meaning writer.

Hotels

French hotels are officially classified on a star system, running from one star to four and *luxe*. (There are also humbler unclassified hotels, not considered as *hôtels de tourisme.*) All hotels show the number of their stars, usually on a plaque by the main entrance. Such stars have nothing to do with Michelin stars. There are thousands of three-star hotels, most of them with restaurants, but there are only about eighteen (the number varies from year to year) Michelin three-star restaurants.

The basis of the star system is somewhat technical. It has to do with the size of the hotel, the proportion of rooms that have private bathrooms, whether there are swimming pools, conference facilities, commissionaires, room service day and night, bars, public rooms and so forth: objective criteria rather than someone's impression of pleasantness. The more stars the dearer, but there is a great deal of overlap according to the room chosen. The top two categories also carry a higher 'luxury' rate of VAT. (The rate is not noticed as such by the customer, the price of the room being always quoted inclusive of VAT and other taxes.)

Room prices are controlled and approved by official bodies such as the Direction Départementale de la Concurrence et des Prix ('County Directorate of Competition and Prices'), and increases caused by improvements to the hotel or a rise in the cost of living need official sanction. Prices are always supposed to be clearly exhibited outside the hotel, showing what one gets for each price, but sometimes one has to go into the hall. The prices are normally shown *service et taxes compris* (*stc* for short – service and tax included). Luxury hotels sometimes quote the service charge separately, as *service 15%* or whatever the rate is in that hotel. Service charges in hotels are not optional. However, in the vast majority of hotels the price exhibited is the total inclusive price, *stc,* and no tip is needed or expected unless one asks for and gets something unusual in the way of help.

It is absolutely normal practice to see the room offered before deciding to take it. All the French do. If it is a very simple hotel, with only one person on duty, perhaps having to be winkled out of the kitchen, you may be given the key and told where the room is, so that you inspect it by yourself. The price of the room is also shown on a card, usually behind the door, together with the price of breakfast and other details.

You pay for the *room*. Most beds are double beds. It is immaterial whether you enjoy your night's stay all by yourself, or whether you let your husband or wife in on the deal. Or your lover, in which case there's no need to call yourselves Mr and Mrs Smith. (Hoteliers like people to come with brand-new lovers: they order better wines at dinner; old married couples rarely want bottles of champagne in the bedroom.) There may be an extra charge if there are more of you. Halfway up France there's a two-star small-town hotel where Sophie and I spend the night en route for London; we always have Room 7, which is about 16' × 18', with private bath and loo; it has two double beds. It cost us £13 in 1985, but if we had been four instead of two it would have been £15. For the room, I repeat, not per person.

This leads us to the point that hotel rooms are better value in France than in Britain, at the time of writing, and I would imagine that this state of affairs will continue. Smaller hotels – one-star and two-star ones, with a dozen rooms – are especially good value, as they are usually run by one family. The French demand and get good salaries for working thirty-nine hours a week with five weeks' holiday a year, but they prefer to be their own bosses. Having conquered their independence they will cheerfully put in eighty hours a week; if they run a hotel it will close down for a mere fortnight, off-season. This competition acts as a constraint on bigger hotels. Of course at the luxury level the sky's the limit. At the Paris Ritz in 1985 it was £18 a night for your little doggie, 15% service and doggie's breakfast not included. Sophie and I haven't been there yet, but we're told you meet a very nice class of chihuahua.

Hotels are understandably reluctant to hold rooms after about 6 p.m. for people who have not sent a deposit. If you telephone to book a room for the night, knowing that you cannot arrive until some later time, you should make sure that the receptionist understands your estimated time of arrival and agrees to hold the room until then. (Immoral tourists have been known to make phone bookings for several hotels for the same night, making their final choice – by inspection of the façade – when they arrive at the town. Early in the evening there is a better chance of re-allocating a room booked by a client who fails to turn up.)

Perhaps because of the fairly low controlled price of rooms, some hotels seem to be asking a lot for breakfast. If this consists of indifferent coffee, a factory-made croissant (croissants are not what they were, unless you find a good baker), a roll, a pat or two of butter wrapped in foil straight out of the fridge so that you can't spread it, and a portion of factory-made jam in a metallic container that you break your fingernails on trying to open, then I object to paying nearly half the price of a modest restaurant lunch for it (the lunch being worth eight times as much, considering the ingredients and labour involved). However, breakfast is not compulsory. Unless one is hooked on breakfasting in the bedroom, a large *café au lait* in a café and a fresh croissant from the baker's can be more satisfactory and better value. But some hotel breakfasts can be delightful.

It seems unbelievable, but British Consuls tell me that Britons are often found wringing their hands in desperation, lost: they have strolled out of their hotel and have no idea what it is called or where it is. . . . Perhaps this happens only to people on package tours, who have been deposited by coach at a hotel chosen by the tour organisers. However, my consular friend asks me to pass on the warning. Almost all hotels have cards on the reception desk, sometimes with a plan of the town, and one can pick one up as one leaves one's key at the desk. (The same apparently happens when people park their cars, if they remember only that it was behind a big brown van and don't look to see the name of the street.)

No pillow? Look in the cupboard and you will probably find one; if not, ask for *un oreiller*. Most French people are content with a bolster (*un traversin*). In a very simple place, if the pillow in the wardrobe has no pillow-slip, this is because they think you will put it under the sheet like a bolster. You could try asking for a pillow-slip (*une taie d'oreiller*).

Soap used not to be provided in the simpler sort of hotel, but now it usually is. It is sensible to travel with one's own soap, just in case. The more modern hotels give one a whole lot of little packets – bubble bath and whatnot. If soapless, ask for *une savonette*: a cake of toilet soap.

Perhaps a set of towels for only one person has been provided in a normal double room. Ask for *des serviettes*.

If there is a little mini-bar fridge, the bottles inside will be over-priced, perhaps to make up for the people who fail to declare what they have consumed. But these mini-bars are handy for keeping one's *own* bottle cool, and the butter and *pâté* from one's picnic bag. . . .

In a small hotel there may be no night porter. If you are going out on the town, ask what the drill is for getting in late (*Je vais rentrer vers minuit – qu'est-ce que je dois faire?*). They might give you the front door key, or show you which bell to ring. It is embarrassing to have to start throwing gravel at windows.

There has recently been a rash of weird modernistic taps operated by one lever like a joystick or gear lever. If there is some arrangement for raising the bath plug by an expensive concatenation of levers and prod-rods, and you can't get it up, you are like me: the weight of the water you have been wallowing in is so great that you have to help to lift the thing off its seating by wiggling a nail file underneath; once the water starts going down the plug-hole all is well.

The red Michelin guide

Any book, French or English, that lists or recommends hotels and restaurants in France should be regarded as an adjunct (often useful, sometimes illuminating, occasionally disastrous) to the Michelin. It is cheese-paring economy to do without it. It costs about the same as a modest meal for one person. Because it contains over 1200 pages of smallish print it might be thought unsuitable for a short motoring holiday near the Channel ports or a little tour by rail, but that would be a mistake. Because of the publicity it gets each year when Foodies rush to see if any of the top twenty-odd world-renowned restaurants have lost a star, and to check other changes in the league table, it tends to be thought of as primarily for gourmets. Not so. They are catered for, certainly. But Michelin does much more. No town, no sizeable village is omitted; there may be no temple of gastronomy there, but Michelin will list a selection of hotels and restaurants throughout the price range; give a town plan whenever the place has more than a couple of dozen streets; tell which garages deal with which cars; give a succinct note of any 'sights', and direct the reader to the local Tourist Information Office. And it is *sérieux*. Criticisms have been levelled at the Michelin guides to Great Britain, Italy and other countries. With the guide to France, one can be sure that half the population takes a look at each year's edition, and if a listed hotel or restaurant deteriorates, letters pour in to the office and are taken seriously. The book is an institution, and the French are its watch-dogs.

I browse in it for pleasure: plans and pipe-dreams. If I were in prison I'd like the current edition, and some old ones going back to the dear old sixties and the far-off thirties, to see who's in, who's out, and to admire the longevity of the great chefs and the little country inns. I'd make imaginary journeys to places I'd never had time to go to: Pussy, for example (Hotel Bellachat, cheap, view of Alps, no dogs in the dining room – well, there wouldn't be, would there?) or Bitche (in the Moselle, nice wine, free garage, dogs welcome) or Revel, or Abondance, or perhaps Dives sur Mer. Should one risk Dizy, Die and Corps? Belley has a starred restaurant. . . .

As with most of the classics, a certain amount of effort is required of the first-time reader. Michelin lists only a selection of the hotels and restaurants in any given town, but even so, and even in a book of over 1200 pages, the only way to include them all is to use a shorthand system of symbols and abbreviations. Eight pages of small print in English (same in French, German and Italian) explain most of them clearly enough, and one really must not try to use such a wonderful but complex instrument without studying those instructions. One needs to take one's time over this, and check one's progress by inspecting a number of entries at random to see if one can extract all the valuable information from the laconic code.

A few points:

- Many towns are named after saints, who in English can be male or female: St John, St Joan. French has *saints*, male, and *saintes*, female. This affects alphabetical order because of the *e*. Michelin (and the telephone directory) uses the convention of putting all the *saints* before all the *saintes*. Thus St Tropez comes *before* Ste Maxime. Not all French lists follow this convention. (Until 1986, the Gault Millau guide went by straight alphabetical order, including of course the *e* of *sainte:* Ste Maxime, St Étienne, St Tropez . . .) Most British-made lists ignore the *e*, producing yet another order. Look again before deciding that a town with a saint's name isn't in the Michelin.
- For alphabetical order *le, la, l'* and *les* are ignored. Le Havre comes under H, les Andelys under A.
- If a town plan is given, the numbered exits correspond to those shown on the yellow Michelin maps, and towns outlined in red on those maps have a corresponding plan in the guide.
- Under the town entry, the post code is given first; or, in the case of a village with no main post office, the post code and name of the post town is given, after an envelope symbol. This should be used when writing to hotels. Also given is the number of the yellow map the town is on, and the number of the fold on that map. The letter *i* stands for the Tourist Information Office (Syndicat d'Initiative, Office de Tourisme). Its address is given, and the dates of opening (but postal enquiries are usually dealt with even when the

office is closed to callers) and its location is shown on the town plan. On these plans a useful symbol is the one showing the permanent market hall. Lots of other town plan symbols, too. . . .

- With hotels, if you have mastered the symbols and abbreviations you should be able to answer these questions (and others): where is the hotel on the town plan? Has it got a car park or garage? Is the garage free to holders of the current guide? Is the hotel quiet? *Exceptionally* quiet? Can one dial long-distance phone calls direct from one's room? Is there air conditioning? Is the place 'modern' (this seems to mean a lot of white formica)? Is there a swimming pool, a tennis court, a spectacular view? Does the price given include service? Which credit cards are accepted? Is there a garden? Are meals served in it? Can one watch the telly in bed, and have breakfast without getting up? Are there rooms accessible for the physically handicapped? All this information and more is given in one line.

- As for restaurants: do not confuse the knife-and-fork symbols and the stars! The more knives and forks, the more luxurious the restaurant; the food will be all right, or the restaurant would not keep its place in the guide. But Foodies go for food, not flunkies, and look for stars.

If the place has one or more stars, the name of the owner, or of the head chef, is given after the name of the restaurant. If he leaves, the stars disappear in the next edition; Michelin re-inspects and considers readers' comments. Keen Foodies check that the chef has not left since the current edition went to press.

Distinguish between the symbol for cheap but satisfactory food and the symbol for good food at a moderate price. Is there a service charge? Is drink included? If not, is wine available cheaply in carafe? Is the cheapest menu served on Sundays and public holidays? (To answer that question you have to look at the size of the type used for the figures.) *Week-ends et fêtes prévenir* means that you probably need to book a table on Sundays and public holidays.

- Prices: if the name of the hotel is given in heavy type (they almost all are) the management has agreed to abide by the prices given, for customers with the current guide. Sometimes the prices are in fact lower. This pleasant surprise occurs because the guide appears in mid-March, but hotels and restaurants have to send their prices to Michelin the previous autumn, and agree to abide by them (unless something awful happens to the national economy). Some protect themselves by over-estimating what they will charge next year. For tourist resorts, high-season prices are given – they will be lower out of season.

  Prices are given for the cheapest room (it might be one of the rare single rooms, too small for a double bed; they are called *single*, a French word used otherwise only for tennis) and for the dearest room; the breakfast charge is given (a black cup when it is served only downstairs, a white cup for breakfast in bed). SC stands for *service compris*, service (and taxes) included.

- Restaurants are listed after hotels. But when looking for a hotel in the guide, look also at the restaurants, because some of them say *avec ch*, short for *avec chambres*: with rooms. These are places that Michelin considers as primarily restaurants. Room prices and details are given as above. Sometimes there are only two or three luxurious and expensive rooms, sometimes they are simpler and cheaper than the dining room might lead one to expect. Such places would not take kindly to your dining elsewhere.

- When are they open? Michelin has not invented symbols to answer this question. It is essential to understand the language, especially in order to avoid travelling to a good restaurant and finding that you have turned up on its weekly day off. These are the key words:

  Days of the week, starting French fashion with Monday: *lundi (lun.), mardi (mar.), mercredi (merc.), jeudi (jeu.), vendredi (ven.), samedi (sam.), dimanche (dim.)*

Months, abbreviated where feasible:
  jan., fév., mars, avril, mai, juin, juil., août, sep., oct., nov., déc.
Also:
  midi – midday
  soir – evening
  fériés – public holidays
  Pâques – Easter
  Pentecôte – Whitsun (the church festival, not the
    British 'spring bank holiday')
  Toussaint – All Saints' Day (1 November)
  Noël – Christmas
  été – summer
  hiver – winter
  vacances scolaires – school holidays
  vacances de février – school half-term holiday at end
    Feb. (Gone ski-ing!)
  hors saison – out of high season
  mi – middle
  fin – end
  fermé – closed
  sauf – exept
  sans rest – no restaurant in this hotel
  week-ends et fêtes prévenir – prudent to book your table
    at weekends and public holidays
Here are some sample entries with expanded translations:
fermé en janv., lundi sauf juil.–août et fériés
closed in January, and on Mondays except during July and
    August and on public holidays (i.e. the place is open
    when a public holiday falls on a Monday)
21 mars–2 oct. et fermé mardi
open from 21 March to 2 October; closed on Tuesdays
fermé mi juil. à fin août et merc.
closed from the middle of July to the end of August, and on
    Wednesdays
fermé mardi soir et merc. sauf vacances scolaires
closed Tuesday evenings and Wednesdays, except during
    school holidays

Pâques–fin sept. et vacances scol. de fév.
open from Easter until the end of September, and during the
February school holidays

I have sometimes found small establishments closed when
they have announced in Michelin that they would be open,
and vice versa, especially in autumn. Hotel-keeping families
cannot always predict their births, marriages and deaths a year
ahead. . . .

Other sources of hotel information

Syndicats d'Initiative and Offices du Tourisme in major towns
(addresses under each town in the Michelin) will send lists of
all hotels in their area, with prices, number of official stars and
basic details. They do like to have an International Reply
Coupon (on sale at British post offices).

There are half a dozen critical guides to hotels and
restaurants, giving fewer entries than the Michelin but
expressing their opinions in short essays. An outstanding one
is the Gault Millau *Guide de la France*, for Foodies (and the
fairly wealthy – it lists some inexpensive restaurants, but one
is constantly distracted by succulent descriptions of what Paul
Bocuse and his many rivals serve to the fortunate gourmets
who booked their table weeks before, turning up fasting,
fighting fit and without a financial care in the world). It lists
only a small selection of hotels, mostly luxurious except when
a modest country inn has caught the compilers' fancy. It is
quicker off the mark for new restaurant talent than the steady
reliable Michelin. It appears in December, dated the
following year, and at present is published only in French.

There are chains of hotels (Frantel, Novotel, Sofitel) listed in
the free *Traveller in France* (French National Tourist Office),
and bookings can be made through a British representative.
Many are relatively expensive town hotels.

France also has a number of groups of independent hotels.
These hotels are not owned and run by a conglomerate; they

agree to conform to certain standards, and benefit by inclusion in the group list. Among these I would single out two groups, one at the luxury end of the market, the other at the one- and two-star level.

The more luxurious one is Relais et Châteaux. Their list is a well-produced booklet with colour photographs, and the French National Tourist Office distributes it in Britain, against payment (in stamps) for postage. As the name implies, the hotels are *châteaux*: country houses and castles. (The best translation of *château* is 'stately home'.) They grade their 100-odd hotels in three levels, from 'exceptionally comfortable with first-class service' to 'comfortable but simple'. ('Simple', here, is about three-star level: elegant and quite expensive by French standards.) The booklet gives a few brief details, but is of course not a critical guide. However, guests are encouraged to send comments to the group's HQ, and there is a form at the back of the booklet for this purpose, so it can be assumed that unsatisfactory establishments are eliminated. (The *relais* are restaurants; some have stars in the Michelin and praise from Gault et Millau, others do not.) A most pleasant tour could be made, staying at peaceful oases of 'gracious living', if one relied mainly on this group. Do get the current year's booklet, so as to plan without disappointment and without surprises at the bill – many of these places are improving their facilities and of course increasing their charges accordingly.

At the Relais et Châteaux level there will be a number of non-French guests, and English, German, etc., will be spoken, but – unlike some big 'international'-type hotels – the atmosphere and the cuisine are satisfactorily French, of the elegant sort.

At the one- and two-star level there is a group that has long given immense satisfaction to those who appreciate the 'real' France. This is Logis et Auberges de France, or Logis for short: nearly 5000 family-run hotels, mostly in the smaller towns, in villages or in the country. Their booklet, with explanations in English and maps, can again be obtained from the London French National Tourist Office, free but not post free. The *auberges* in the booklet are simpler than the *logis*, often not having enough rooms for them to be classified officially as *hôtels de tourisme* – i.e. not even one official star; but they can be splendidly friendly places, basic as far as bedroom fittings go but superb value in the dining room for those who go native with gusto. Prices are of course given in the booklet, always inclusive of service, etc. As with Relais et Châteaux, you are encouraged to send comments to HQ. Places that drop their standards are eliminated.

Michelin is comprehensive: it covers all France. Logis, being a voluntary grouping, is not. Some areas have lots of *logis*, presumably because hotels find it a good thing and pass the word to the neighbours. Other parts, including some of my favourite regions where excellent small hotels abound, have not a single *logis* for miles, simply because the idea has not caught on locally. It would be a pity to draw negative conclusions about an area because there are no *logis* there.

There are other hotel groups listed in the French National Tourist Office's handouts, but if one is pottering around France in a car, free as air, there is a limit to the number of reference books one wants to consult. For hotels, I suggest Michelin and either *Relais et Châteaux* or *Logis* according to taste and finances. Or all three of them: Sophie and I have a two-star income, but instead of leading an unvarying two-star life, we find it pleasant to have two or three nights at a simple level and then a 2 p.m. to 11 a.m. spell among the peacocks and swimming pools, with a bathroom to swing a pedigree cat in. No point in going to such places just to sleep. . . . The cost averages out.

Why am I not naming any English books that recommend hotels and restaurants? First, because the ones that I have looked at in 1985 will be unreliable in 1986, and I have no notion what hot-from-the-press English book will be published then, nor in 1987, nor later; what I suggest the reader should have is the Michelin and perhaps the Gault Millau and/or *Logis de France*, and if they don't keep on appearing yearly, revised and re-researched and criticised by millions of pernickety French people until the year 2000 and later, I shall burst into tears. Secondly, such English books are usually produced by talented individuals, whereas Michelin, etc., are the work of expert teams. There is a limit to the number of meals an individual can eat in a year, and the number of beds he can sleep in. Thirdly, such books can list only a much smaller number of places than the French guides, and this can lead to finding the dining room full of one's compatriots. Such a state of affairs, common enough near the Channel ports, is of ill omen as regards food, service and value (which might well have been excellent before the British, and especially alas the British child, scared the locals away and corrupted the boss. I know of one restaurant near Calais that puts the British in a separate dining room. ...)

Restaurants

No purple patches, says Sophie. Don't go starry-eyed. This is a plain down-to-earth book for practical people. Right then.

Rotten, over-priced restaurants do exist in France. We found one in 1964. Since then we have sometimes had meals at ostensibly low prices that turned out to be perfunctory as food, sloppily served and not worth the money. Those were all in spots where tourists gather; the last was in the big square at Avignon near the Palace of the Popes, and hardly a customer was French. Our fault – we were in a hurry, and we wanted to sit out in the open under a parasol. Avignon is in fact an excellent town for restaurants, but we hadn't got our Michelin or our Gault Millau, and anyway we were going to be taken out that evening to a good restaurant (dinner was delicious and cost our hosts only 50 per cent more a head than our lunch – Hiély, described later, would have been 300 per cent more).

Fortunately, the French have a tradition of eating out fairly frequently. If they are commercial travellers or other workers who cannot go home at midday for a two-hour lunch break, they want to repair the ravages of getting up at six and doing a morning's work without a tea-break, so they give earnest attention to a properly prepared meal. And most French families eat out together regularly. That is why Sunday lunch sees restaurants full; often a special menu is put on, at an extra charge. The fact that restaurants in France, from temples of gastronomy to simple family-run places, are among the country's major attractions is a tribute to the native customer; we can have confidence in his keen seriousness in the matter, bless him. All classes contribute: the rich have better food and drink, and luxury items appear more often on their tables, but attitudes are essentially similar – unlike in Britain, even today. I ate with the horny-handed workers at a factory canteen recently: avocado for starters, roast quail, chips, French beans, Camembert, a pear; quite good wine . . . Perhaps my fellow-lunchers would not appreciate the more extreme manifestations of *la nouvelle cuisine*, but that has almost had its day. I think it started up only because Henri Gault and Christian Millau were getting seriously overweight.

PRICES

So long as present well-established patterns and regulations persist there should be no surprises. All French restaurants, great and small, exhibit priced menus outside the door. There might be an *à la carte* list, with all dishes individually priced, and three or four fixed-price menus of three to seven courses. Small family-run places might have just one menu, offering excellent value for simple (by French standards) food bought – in the best cases – that morning at the market by the cook, or gathered from the garden.

However, there are two matters to bear in mind if one wants to make an accurate forecast of the bill: service and drinks. (TVA, French for VAT, is always included in the prices shown.)

Service: in the majority of restaurants today the menu outside clearly states *service compris* (SC in the Michelin guide). This means that there is no service charge to add on as it is included in the price, and no tip is expected or should be offered (unless one has received some exceptional treatment). It is at the more expensive restaurants that there is a service charge, and again this will be clearly shown: *service 12%*, or 15%, or whatever. This will be added to the bill, and is not optional.

Liquid refreshment: there are four possible situations. (1) and (2) below both come under the indication *bc* (*boisson comprise*) in the Michelin guide. See 'Wine in restaurants', page 177.

1) *Vin compris* can mean that you have as much ordinary wine as you want, 'free' with the menu (but not, of course, expensive wine from the wine list, *la carte des vins*). Other drinks – beer, mineral water, etc. – will be extra.

2) *Boisson comprise* means 'drink included'. What you get 'free' is clearly shown. It might be a choice from a quarter-litre carafe or *pichet* (jug) of ordinary wine, a bottle of beer and a bottle of mineral water. Further supplies must be paid for.

3) Wine may be available, quite cheaply, in carafe or *pichet*. (The smallest *pichet* holds *un quart*, a quarter of a litre.) Michelin indicates this with a carafe symbol. Other drinks are at normal restaurant prices.

4) If none of the above applies, the wine will be expensive – in 1986 prices, say 40 francs a bottle with the 70-franc menu. In such cases the price of wine might not be stated outside. This almost always happens at expensive restaurants. If Michelin seems to suggest that you can eat well at the Ritz for 400 francs, you have not learned to read that guide properly. There is no SC shown, nor of course is there a carafe symbol or *bc*. Gault et Millau suggest 500 francs, because they are counting the 15 per cent service charge and a modest ration of wine.

A jug of tap water must, by law, be provided free. If it is not on the table, ask: *de l'eau, s'il vous plaît*. If the response is *de l'eau minérale?*, and you don't want to pay for a bottle of Vichy or other water (*gazeuse*, fizzy, or *plate*, still) say *non, une carafe d'eau, s'il vous plaît*. In the case of the 70-franc restaurant in (4) above, if the menu seems to represent outstanding value (usually in a restaurant in a prominent touristic spot) this might make you slightly unpopular; you might even, sadly, get less generous portions. The place counts on the drinks bill for its main profits. If you really like tap water, cases (1), (2) and (3) are more suitable.

Beer will be willingly served – the posher the restaurant the posher the brand, priced accordingly.

Coca-Cola, etc., with meals: yes, priced as beer. Recommended only if you are under eight years old and do not mind being regarded as a barbarous child. It does not go with French food.

Coffee and tea are optional extras after a meal. *Un café* is a small black coffee. Medium-priced and expensive restaurants are taking to charging a high price for it, and serving it with *petits fours* and/or a few elegant sweets. If your French is very good you might succeed in getting breakfast-style *café-au-lait* served *with* your meal. But you will be regarded as stark raving bonkers; pitying smiles will be exchanged around you. Quite right, too. You are insulting the food.

Some restaurants propose *apéritifs*, at about double the café price, usually including 'free' interesting little home-made nibbles (*des amuse-gueules*) to go with them. These can be nice, and good value, all in all, but they are by no means compulsory. I prefer, if I am ordering a bottle of white wine to go with the *hors d'oeuvre* and the fish, to ask for it to be served *tout de suite*, to sip while waiting.

THE ROUTINE

Choice among restaurants that fall within one's price range should not, of course, be made solely on inspection of the menu. If the restaurant is in the Michelin guide at all, never mind about stars, it is safe. If it goes off, Michelin receives dozens of complaints from the French, and re-inspects. This is why Michelin's guide to France is more reliable than their guides to other countries' restaurants. I repeat that the presence of apparently local customers is a good sign. And in the summer, if there are tables outside, one may even be able to observe what people are eating before one reaches the point of no return.

If the restaurant is one of the very limited number of two- or three-star places in the Michelin guide, or has three or four *toques* (Gault et Millau's equivalent of the Michelin stars) in Gault Millau, you will almost certainly need to book. Despite the price, the *salle* ought to be full, unless something awful has happened since the guide went to press. One also may need to book at cheaper restaurants, if they offer very good value. 'I'd like to book a table for two for half-past twelve today/tomorrow' – *Je voudrais réserver une table pour deux, pour midi et demi aujourd'hui/demain.*

On entering, hang around expectantly until a table is allocated. Empty tables may have been reserved.

In any decent restaurant, including the cheapest, a fairly lengthy discussion when the menu is presented is quite in order (just watch the French). Some English people are too diffident about taking up the time of the staff in this important operation. They do want you to enjoy your meal; questions will be answered, explanations given, and when practicable, dishes may even be shown. Choice of dessert can be left until later, but the main strategy is planned at the beginning, and a conscientious boss (it is usually a senior figure who takes the order) will point out if the second course you are considering does not really harmonise with the main dish.

Bread will be brought, but not butter. Butter makes its appearance only with raw ham, radishes and oysters. There are enough fats in the food, especially in the sauces (unless it is *nouvelle cuisine*); bread is plain neutral padding to accompany juicy richness. In Normandy and some other parts, a couple of ounces of butter may have gone into the plateful, or the equivalent in cream. . . .

The restaurant bill is *l'addition* (f.). (A hotel bill, for rooms, etc., is *une note*; all other bills, for car repairs, for example, are *des factures*, f.)

LANGUAGE AND FOOD; MORE ABOUT RESTAURANTS

First-timers in France who know no French have adventures awaiting them. With average luck, most of them should be pleasant, or at least interesting. A descriptive vocabulary of French food would fill a fat volume, since in many cases there is no English translation – a recipe is required. I heartily recommend studying, during long winter evenings, a book like Elizabeth David's *French Provincial Cooking*, even if one is never going to boil a single egg; one learns what it is all about, including the words. Food does not translate, anyway. The British have learnt to make omelettes, and some of them can make mayonnaise; those are French words, and no pedant has tried to invent English ones to take their places. (Folded disc of eggs? Olive oil and yolk emulsion?) If one likes *moules marinières* one might as well think of them as *moules marinières* rather than 'mussels in seamanlike style'.

Complete beginners, if wealthy, should start at the top. At world-renowned restaurants and luxury hotels staff are used to American millionaires with no language except their native dialect; and the restaurants also cater for English gourmets. The latter, some of whom may have a shaky command of French, have a reputation as connoisseurs; so the customer who needs to have most things explained in English is well catered for in every respect.

If they are not wealthy, they would do well to start near the bottom, in good, simple, family-run restaurants. There, they will meet the basic traditional dishes – in French, as it is less likely that anyone speaks English well enough to give an adequate description of them. After the beginner has cut his teeth, as it were, on sound family fare, and knows from experience the difference between a *fricassée* and a *daube*, he will have enough restaurant French to attempt more elaborate menus in the middle range of restaurants.

The standard unimaginative French meal, corresponding to tomato soup, slices from the joint and two veg. followed by something-and-custard in Britain, revolves around *bifteck-frites*, steak and chips; acceptable everywhere from works canteen to posh restaurant. If the steak is just called *bifteck* it will come from some part of the animal that yields chewable meat; better quality cuts will be called *bavette, onglet, faux-filet, entrecôte, rumstek* or *filet*, in that order of tenderness and price. You will always be expected to say how you want it done: rare or nearly raw is *saignant* (bleeding); medium is *à point*, pink in the middle; well done is *bien cuit*. If you do not like underdone meat, *bien cuit* will often seem nearer what one might in Britain call medium: the French prefer their meat under-cooked, and indeed prolonged cooking toughens the cheaper cuts. The *bifteck-frites* will be preceded by *hors d'oeuvre* and followed by *salade*, plain green salad with oil and vinegar provided; then cheese, *le fromage*, and then *la tarte aux fruits*, fruit tart – or some other *pâtisserie*. In a really cheap place it will be *fromage* OU *dessert*, cheese OR sweet. This standard meal can turn out to be delicious or very humdrum. In the evening *le potage*, soup, usually a vegetable soup (not from a tin) takes the place of *hors d'oeuvre*. (The word *soupe*, otherwise a slang word corresponding to 'grub', usually occurs only as *soupe à l'oignon* or *soupe de poissons* (onion soup, fish soup), fairly substantial dishes involving grated cheese, sometimes eaten as complete meals.)

It might be useful to attempt a running commentary on some genuine menus:

RESTAURANT A is a simple place in a small town in the Midi. The dining room seats about sixty; but a hundred can be served in summer, when tables go out on the terrace under the plane trees. Lunch starts soon after 12 p.m.; by 12.45 p.m. there may be no more room. One sitting; you need at least an hour and a half to eat here. Fewer people in the evening. One menu only:

Menu du . . . (date; the menu changes every day, according to what Madame A. buys and what is in season)
Déjeuner à F62,00 (this was 1985), *vin et service compris:* no service charge, no tip expected; here, *vin compris* means litre bottles of decent local red wine on every table. When one

bottle is empty, another appears as if by magic; no limit. Water on table; bottled mineral water extra. Beer is 8 francs for a small bottle. No charge for a *couvert* for a small child – i.e. a plate and cutlery are provided, and the child eats free from its parents' portions.

First Course *hors d'oeuvre variés: variés* means that the *hors d'oeuvre* includes meaty things; if exclusively raw vegetables – grated carrot, celeriac, etc. – they might just be called *crudités*. Here, this course is generous: the usual *crudités*, plus home-made pâté – the terrine is left on the table, cut and come again – *saucisson sec*, and another kind of salami, anchovies, olives . . . one could make a good light meal from this course alone, but it's either the menu or nothing.

Second Course *langue de boeuf, sauce piquante OU petite friture OU jambon de montagne*: hot ox tongue in a piquant sauce, or 'whitebait', i.e. tiny local fresh fish deep-fried whole and served sizzling, or raw mountain ham, a couple of slices with pats of butter.

Third Course (but in fact served with the next course) *asperges OU haricots verts OU pommes sautées:* fresh local asparagus or French beans or sautéed potatoes.

Fourth Course *rôti de boeuf OU rôti de veau OU poulet rôti*: roast beef or veal or chicken; the thick slice of beef will be underdone for most British tastes, but ask for it to be *bien cuit* and they will show it to the fire again – this is a family place and they're not happy if the customer looks dismal.

Fifth Course *fromages*: help yourself from a big cheese board, about six sorts, some good – Roquefort is often there, it's almost local.

Sixth Course *fruit OU glace*: a choice from the fruit bowl, or a factory-made ice-cream. This place does not go in for elaborate desserts.

And there you are, and 62 francs is the bill, no more, no less. Coffee extra, but we usually go somewhere else for that. Not bad at about £5.50, wine included. The staple customers are commercial travellers and local workers, who got up at six or earlier and had a light breakfast; after lunch here they can carry on until 8 p.m. Holiday-makers who rose at nine are often overwhelmed by the copiousness; if not, they find that a light snack in the evening is all they need.

At Sunday lunch (well attended) the menu is F85, with 'nobler' dishes: salmon, perhaps, for the second course, or sole; quails or guinea-fowl or something else superior for the fourth course; a meal for celebrations, not just for keeping going. But still *vin compris, service compris.*

The service can be slow when there are a lot of customers; Sophie and I go there when we have visitors and things to discuss, so a couple of hours passes quickly.

I had a talk with Madame A:

'Is it hard work, running a place like this?'

'Well, some people would think so. This is a hotel as well, you see. Either my husband or I keep busy from half-past six in the morning until shutting-up time at night, and often both of us. We employ eight people, some of them part time, including a nice girl who comes in to do the paperwork – what with credit cards and VAT and the rest, I'm glad to get that off my shoulders. All the work is done here, even the laundry.'

'What about days off?'

'The staff get the regulation rest days and holidays, but we open seven days a week, three hundred and sixty-five days a year, so I'm always working.'

'Do you mind that?'

'Perhaps you won't believe me, but I just love it. I really do! I like to keep busy, but the main thing is the personal contact. I like meeting new people, and I love my old customers, the ones who've been coming here all their lives. They tell me their troubles, they come for their wedding banquets and their children's ... Oh, I've got hundreds of friends! And not just in this town – not long ago our daughter went and stayed with an English family who often come here.'

'Do you get many foreigners?'

'Quite a few in the summer, especially now they've opened that big campsite down by the lake. You'll think I'm saying this because you're English, but it's the truth – the English are my favourite foreigners. They've got such a sense of humour. Let's not name names, but some foreigners are so solemn and uptight ... not the English. And the English love French food. At any rate, the ones who take their holidays in this area, away from the tourist places. And I will say this, you get good home cooking here. Not a scrap of deep-frozen stuff crosses my door. If there's no nice fish in the market, there's no fish on the menu.'

RESTAURANT B is in a bigger town (8000 inhabitants) in the same region. The town is nearer the sea, and attracts visitors because of its unspoilt Renaissance quarter; the restaurant is part of a modest hotel (Logis de France) and is quite well known as a comfortable night stop en route to and from Spain. It is in the Michelin guide, but it has no star or red R (the red R signifies Michelin's recommendation of good meals at moderate prices).

Three menus: 50 francs, 75 francs and 100 francs, and an *à la carte* list. *Service compris,* but *boisson non comprise.* However, a quarter-litre jug of local *vin rouge* or *rosé* costs F3,50, about 30p. A small bottle of *eau minérale* costs 6 francs, same size beer 9 francs. Full list of superior wines.

The 50-franc menu is rather like the menu of Restaurant A, cut down: *hors d'oeuvre variés* (less copious, a little more elegant), OR *pâté à l'Armagnac* (a superior pâté with brandy among the ingredients) OR *omelette aux fines herbes;* then *côte de porc grillée* (grilled pork chop) OR *poulet rôti* (roast chicken) OR *saucisse grillée* (sausage) – served with *pommes frites* (chips) OR *épinards à la crème* (creamed spinach) OR *salade verte* (lettuce, which is what *salade* normally means in French – anything with bits of tunny fish, etc., in it is *une salade composée,* and served as a first course); then *fromage* (wider selection than in Restaurant A) OR *dessert,* of which there is a reasonable choice (tarts, ice-cream, sorbets).

The 75-franc menu takes us to a more advanced linguistic level:

First Course *filets de hareng fumé avec pommes en salade*: smoked herring fillets, rather like kipper, cold, with potato salad OR *pâté à l'Armagnac* OR *escargots de pays, façon Suzanne*: S.'s way of doing small local snails – in a spicy sauce OR *baudroie pêcheur*: monkfish – pieces of it in a kind of soup OR *moules à l'américaine*: mussels, in shell, in tomato, cream and brandy sauce.

Second Course *calamars en civet*: squid stew (*calamars* is just another name for *encornets*) OR *langue de veau, sauce aux câpres*: calf's tongue, hot, with caper sauce OR *demi coquelet grillé*: half a baby chicken – literally, a small cockerel OR *brochette de rognons et de ris de veau*: grilled skewer of kidney and calf's sweetbreads OR *noix d'entrecôte vigneronne (supplt F18)*: eye of rib steak with 'female vine-grower's' sauce, i.e. a wine sauce, at 18 francs extra charge OR *cassolette languedocienne (supplt F18)*: various items of seafood, hot, in a little pot, with flaky pastry on top; extra charge . . . all the above being served *garni*, i.e. with vegetable accompaniment: *pommes frites* OR *légumes de saison* (veg. in season – one asks what is on offer) OR *salade verte*.

Third Course *plateau de fromages*: excellent selection; unlike on the 50-franc menu, we have cheese AND . . .

Fourth Course *dessert*

The 100-franc menu is still 'nobler', and *à la carte* there are specialities from 40 francs to 90 francs per portion.

Some English is spoken, and Madame B is kind and helpful. An English family of beginners could do well with 75-franc menus for grown-ups and 50-franc ones for children. No charge for a small child's *couvert*, if it will eat from others' helpings (the chip ration is more than generous . . .). I had a chat with Madame B, at 10 a.m., in the quiet moment between clearing away the breakfasts and getting started on lunch preparations.

'Were you born into the hotel-restaurant business?'

'No, I married into it. The hotel opened in 1787 as a coaching inn – your Arthur Young stayed here soon after – but my late husband's family took it over four generations ago.'

'Do you get many English people?'

'Oh yes, we get all nationalities and all sorts. Lots of locals, too. We have a good cheap menu, but you can spend a lot if you want to. We get workmen, commercial travellers, executives . . . We had a British ambassador once – not the present one.'

'Is it hard work?'

'I'm on the go, more or less, from six in the morning till eleven at night. But we're shut on Mondays, and for three weeks in November. I look after the hotel side, run the dining room and do most of the marketing. Apart from deep-frozen frogs' legs and giant prawns, we buy our stuff fresh every day or almost. My son is the chef; he's had proper professional training. And my mother helps behind the scenes. We have quite a few paid staff, and an accountant comes in to do the taxes. I like my work – people are fascinating.'

'Any national differences?'

'To some extent. The Swiss and the Dutch can be a little difficult – they know just how they want things, and can make a fuss if it's not just right. Some of the English are timid. They tend to stick to chicken and chips. Do you have asparagus in England? You know, you pick it up in your fingers by the tough white end, dip it in the sauce and just eat the tender part? We had an English family who were using knives and forks and trying to chew chunks off the wrong end. I plucked up my courage and showed them how to manage. There are some things you just have to eat in your fingers, like *écrevisses* (fresh-water crayfish) – we do them in a brandy-and-tomato sauce, and we tie a bib round customers' necks and give them a finger-bowl afterwards. There were some Americans here the other day. They drank a lot of spirits before they started eating, and then asked for milky coffee with their meat! Well I never! We gave them what they wanted, but there are places that wouldn't. Food and wine are meant to go together, and this is a wine district – the local wine we serve in *pichets* is quite good.'

Sophie and I eat there when we happen to be in the town. If we have a lot to do in the afternoon we have the cheap lunch menu. It isn't exciting, but it's quite good; we're in and out in only an hour, and we don't feel we need to go and lie down afterwards to digest, unlike with Restaurant A. (There, despite resolutions to skip a course, we always over-eat.) But if we have time, we take the 75-franc menu. There are always new things on it, so we experiment. Sometimes one of us has that menu, and the other just has an expensive dish *à la carte*, starting with a salad; then Sophie has the menu's cheese and I have its pudding.

There are half a dozen other restaurants in the town, not in the Michelin guide but quite adequate. Restaurant B is in a poor position: on the main road with only the narrowest of pavements in front. The other day I saw a new restaurant in a good location to attract tourists: attractive printed menus, not hand-written (rigid 'efficient' catering?). Restaurant B's prices, at first sight – but nothing about *vin* or *boisson*, no indication of carafe wine, and *service à l'appréciation du client*, which just means service charge not included, so if one doesn't give at least 10 per cent one will be made to feel a miser. I don't think I'll try it.

Restaurants A and B are in the Hérault *département*. Not one of France's most favoured restaurant *départements*, it has few red Rs or stars in the Michelin. Elsewhere, comparable meals can be cheaper, and better ones no dearer. A study of Michelin's 'red R' and 'star' maps is illuminating: where stars cluster, unstarred restaurants can be very good because of the competition.

Let us now move upwards to the Advanced Level. At Avignon there is a temple of gastronomy: the Restaurant Hiély. It can do no harm to mention it by name; it's far from undiscovered. Michelin gives it two stars for food, and three knives and forks for comfort. Gault et Millau award three *toques* (four is their maximum) and seventeen marks out of twenty. Madame Hiély reigns over the dining room, at the head of a smart band

87

of waiters and waitresses. It's not a big restaurant and one usually needs to book. Monsieur Hiély is *au piano*, as they say: in the kitchen, with expert helpers. The Hiélys run things smoothly and have high standards; when they take a rest (three weeks in the summer, a fortnight in the winter, every Tuesday and most Mondays) the restaurant is shut. Nothing to see from the street, except a door (the restaurant is upstairs) and the menu – a model of rigorous clarity. It changes frequently, according to what is in season and what new dishes Pierre Hiély creates. Expensive, but one can see in a moment, standing in the street, what one will have to pay. No surprises when *l'addition* arrives.

Here we go:

A l'apéritif particulièrement recommandé:
Notre Champagne Sélection, la bouteille: 230 f.
Le Kir Hiély: 24 f.
Champagne Framboise: 38 f.
(*Kir* is white wine with a shot of blackcurrant liqueur; *champagne framboise* is a cocktail unknown to me. If I were in a party of four I might suggest sharing a bottle of the house champagne. But an *apéritif* is quite optional. Sophie and I have lunched here twice, and each time we started on our meal-time wine while waiting for the first course, nibbling the interesting *amuse-gueules* on the table.)

Notre menu à 210 f. Service compris 15%
(This is 1986 . . . The service charge is included in the price – the Hiélys are just letting you know what the staff get, by quoting 15%.)

Brouillade de Corail d'Oursins en Croustade: brouillade is scrambled egg; it is mixed with the orange part extracted from sea-urchins – *oursins* – and served *en croustade*, in puff pastry. That would be an adventurous choice; I recommend it.

Paupiette de Saumon au Noilly: this is nearer home – salmon lightly baked in a paper or foil case, perfumed with Noilly Prat vermouth.

Vinaigrette Tiède d'Aile de Raie et de Saint-Jacques: shreds of wing of skate – skate *is* a good fish, properly done – and scallops – they are *coquilles Saint-Jacques* – served *tiède,* luke-warm, in a vinaigrette sauce.

Ragoût de Nouilles Fraîches, Goujonnettes de Soles et Palourdes, Coulis de Poivrons Doux: now that's nice. A mixture of fresh noodles, little bits of sole and carpet-shell cockles, in a purée of sweet peppers.

Foie Gras Frais de Canard des Landes (suppl. + 20): fresh *foie gras* – duck, not the more usual goose – from the *département* of the Landes; 20 francs extra, though.

Then the twelve choices for today's second course. Here are some:

Pintadeau de Ferme à la Feuille de Chou et au Bacon (2 personnes): small free-range – *mais naturellment!* – guinea-fowl, roasted in a wrapping of cabbage leaves with slivers of the lean part of 'best back' bacon; for two people – the bird is of course freshly roasted, and comes whole; the waiter carves.

Turbotin au Vin Rouge, Julienne de Poireaux à la Crème: turbot poached in *red* wine, rather unusual, with shredded leeks in cream.

Pieds et Paquets Provençale: see page 141 for canned version. Never had sheep's tripe? Delicious!

Médaillon de Foie de Veau à la Moutarde et aux Câpres: calf's liver in mustard and caper sauce.

Coeur de Filet à la Moelle aux Echalottes (suppl. + 12): heart of fillet steak, with beef marrow and shallots, 12 francs extra.

(Of course one chooses one's two courses so that they will go together. Madame Hiély takes the order. She speaks English, and will explain, as far as such things can be explained.)

Fromages

Dessert

Surprisingly laconic! A good selection of cheese — and then *what* a pudding course. .... Enormous choice, all home made of course. A splendid 'ice-cream cake' — ice-cream, meringue, etc. — and all kinds of unusual sorbets. Second helpings encouraged — oh, the temptation. ....

Nos Vins de Carafe	75cl	50cl	35cl
Tavel rosé	66	44	33
Châteauneuf-du-Pape	86	58	43

(Another surprise, at a restaurant of this elegance, is carafe wine. Not cheap, compared with F3,50 for 25cl at Restaurant B, but these are very good wines. No carafe symbol in the Michelin guide, because of their price.)

That's what you see on the menu. By the side there is the wine list. The cheapest here is a Coteaux de Languedoc (a good one, I know it) at 80 francs, slightly cheaper than the carafe red above. There are well over a hundred wines on the list; plenty at between 100 and 200 francs, rising through a 1976 Échézeaux at 420 francs to a 1945 Château Margaux at 1200 francs, a 1904 Château d'Yquem at 1900 francs and a 1947 Volnay Santenots at 2200 francs. Sophie and I found that 44 francs' worth of rosé and 58 francs' worth of red, in carafe, was quite adequate. We've only been twice. If this book becomes a best-seller we'll go again — they have some very nice magnums of vintage claret (of course we shall phone the day before to book the table and get the bottle stood upright).

A typical top restaurant? There are no typical ones. An unusual thing here is the formula: one menu, with a wide choice. Other restaurants of this class tend to have only an *à la carte* list. The formula makes Hiély relatively cheap, at its level. Is this sort of thing worth it? In theory, Sophie and I would rather spend the money on books — on the other hand, there are some feasts we remember with joy, twenty years later. ....

Chapter 9

The café

What an admirable institution the café is! How pleasant to sit in the sun, or in the shade of a multicoloured parasol advertising *apéritifs*, or under a pergola of wisteria, sipping one's cool lager and keeping an eye on life's passing show, while one's near and dear toy with ice-creams, lemonade from a freshly squeezed lemon (*le citron pressé*) or even a rashly ordered little pot of tea-bag tea! Or to scuttle in under a sudden shower, whether at 9.30 a.m. or p.m., at tea-time or at midnight. . . .

Of course it isn't what it was. Every home has television now, and the habit of using the local café twice a day as a sort of extra drawing room for meeting friends or customers or professional contacts, or for writing novels several hours daily at one's regular table like Sartre and Simone de Beauvoir, has passed into social history. In our nearest small town the cafés do good business only in the summer months, when the tables come out under the plane trees in the avenue, and then half the customers are 'foreigners' – Parisians, Britons and such . . . And the drinks have got rather dear, by earlier standards.

As for prices: a list should be clearly visible. Some cafés might seem outrageously expensive, others relatively cheap – for precisely the same items (or apparently so – a posh place's *pastis* will be the same liquid as a cheap place's, but its cognac will be better). This is natural. As I shall suggest, one goes to a café to spend a much longer time per drink than in a British pub. Seats in the dress circle of a theatre are dearer than those in the gallery, but the chocolates are just the same. I sometimes do a little examining in Toulouse. If I just want a cup of good coffee after dinner, I get it at a little place in a side street. But on a fine evening I sit at a table on the terrace of an elegant café on the Place Wilson (Woodrow, not Harold) overlooking the fountains. I pay twice the price. I read my book, looking up every few minutes to observe charming young ladies as they stroll; I listen discreetly to indiscreet conversations at neighbouring tables; I write a letter to Sophie; an hour and a half goes in a flash, and I have paid a negligible price for my accommodation. In a French café the price of admission is one *consommation,* and you are normally welcome to make it last a long long time.

Drinks at the table are a little dearer than drinks at the counter (but in many cafés you can't drink at the counter anyway). You pay when you leave, not when the *serveur* or *serveuse* brings your order. When you want to leave you attract his or her attention. But if one *serveur* goes off duty, to be replaced by another, the one who took your order will come to ask for the money (the amount is clearly stated on a little chit, and please don't let it blow away) because he is personally responsible for collecting it, and if you slip away forgetting to pay, it is he who will be out of pocket. However, in busy seasons, and in tourist spots where there are a lot of foreigners, the *serveur* will have to ask for the money when he brings the order. He is addressed, by the way, as *monsieur,* not *garçon* (and she is *madame* or *mademoiselle,* whichever you think would please her).

Usual drinks: mineral water (Vichy, Perrier, etc.); various coloured *sirops* (mint, *menthe*; *grenadine,* etc.) diluted with water, much favoured by the impecunious young; coffee: *un café* is a small black coffee; white coffee is *un café crème* or *un café au lait* – *grand* or *petit;* the former is usual at breakfast time, when *croissants* and probably bread, butter and jam will be available – *un petit déjeuner;* ice-creams, elaborate or paper-wrapped, according to the pretensions of the place; and beer (*une pression* is draught beer; see page 191); perhaps wine (see page 173).

A favourite low-alcohol thirst-quencher in the south is *un pastis* (Pernod, Ricard, etc.), that greenish aniseedy drink that, like Dettol, turns cloudy when you pour water in it. It may seem odd to call it a low-alcohol drink, as it is the same strength as whisky, but it is served in very small shots at the bottom of a glass devised to make the amount look bigger, and is served with a jug of iced water: dilute, sip, re-dilute. One grows to like *pastis,* when it's hot and the cicadas are chirping and the *pétanque* balls are clinking.

All the usual stronger drinks (whisky, cognac, etc.) are available, served in biggish shots at a much higher price than the popular *pastis.* Also, *apéritifs* like Martini and Dubonnet; inferior port (*le porto*) but not sherry (well, you can try, at some fashionable place in Paris: *le sherry,* or *le vin de Xérès*).

The café should be used for its proper purpose, as a sort of hotel where one stays for at least half an hour enjoying the social, sanitary and aesthetic facilities. It is not a watering-hole for a thirsty family unless they have money to throw around. A journalist recently wrote an excellent article on a bicycle ride he made in 1984, from the centre of France to the Atlantic coast. On one hot day, he said, he spent 100 francs on Orangina (quite a good orange drink). It is obvious that he absorbed this liquid in the form of little 25cl bottles at cafés, at about 8 francs the bottle, or 32 francs the litre. So he had about three litres, by no means too much for a cyclist on a hot day. Three litres of fizzy orange or lemon, bought in litre bottles at *épiceries,* would have cost him about 10 francs. ... Perhaps he wanted to stop at a dozen different cafés, perhaps it was all on the expense account, or perhaps he didn't have room on his bike. Four or five people in a car, instead of one man on a saddle, will find it more sensible to avoid dehydration with the help of a cool-box and a few plastic cups. Thirsty children should be regularly watered, but not at two-minute café stops. Buy Pschitt, Sic or Coca-Cola in litre bottles. A fifty-fifty mixture of Valstar beer and Pschitt lemonade makes a nice shandy (*un panaché*) and the do-it-yourself version, under the trees by the roadside, is cheaper than in French cafés or anywhere in Britain.

Café loos: please do not treat these as free public conveniences. The facilities are for the use of customers, as in Britain. A coffee does not cost much.

Chapter 10

Snacks and picnics

France is a more convenient country than Britain for finding
proper sit-down meals: proper food at proper times. Proper
means French, of course. People who do not much mind what
they eat and would rather get on with some other activity are
less well provided for than in Britain, where snack bars,
hamburger joints and pizzerias abound, where most pubs can
provide a sandwich or a reconstituted shepherd's pie, and
where Chinese restaurants serve Menu A at any time of the
day.

However, *le fast-food* has made its appearance. One can get
un Big-Mac or something like it at branches of Macdonald's,
What-a-Burger, Free-Time and other places in big towns.
These are mainly patronised by the young, and frowned
upon by most of their elders on gastronomic, dietetic and
(especially) linguistic grounds. Big towns also have fairly
authentic pizzerias; *crêperies* (pancake houses) under Breton
influence and a few Chinese restaurants – though these are
often Indo-Chinese (Vietnam was a French possession once)
and are unlikely to serve quick meals outside normal eating

hours. Cafés are less than satisfactory for snacks, on the whole. The French sandwich is dull (ham, cheese or pâté – *le sandwich au jambon, au fromage, au pâté*) and, since it is a cylinder of French bread, one needs both hands and widely opening jaws. Cafés sometimes offer *un croque-monsieur*: a toasted sandwich of ham in British-type sliced wrapped bread, rather dear for what one gets – and anyway most of the above items are poor value compared with a modestly priced proper meal at the proper time in a proper place.

A word of praise, though, for the cafeterias at some hypermarkets (Casino, for example). The choice is good, the surroundings are better than at comparable British places, and some of the food, like steak, is freshly cooked – and served at any time from (in some cafeterias) 11 a.m. to 11 p.m. For a steak you will be asked if you want it *saignant* (bleeding), *à point* (medium, but on the rare side) or *bien cuit* (well done), and given a numbered disc. Take the rest of your meal through the cash-point, pay for it all, and when they sing your number out your steak is ready. Wine by the jug for a few pence. Not bad.

It is not disgracefully wicked to prefer, occasionally, a snack meal to a proper meal, and noon to 2 p.m. can be a good time to cover the distance on the roads, which are deserted by proper eaters. Museums and *châteaux* may well be closed at that time, and most shops except hypermarkets, but hills and rivers and beaches are still there, and town architecture. The best way to have a snack meal in France is to have a picnic, and France not only has better weather for picnicking, usually – it is also a wonderful country for buying picnic food. I would strongly advise anyone going to France with a car to take a good set of picnic equipment: plates, knives, including at least one sharp one for carving, things to drink out of, corkscrew and bottle-opener of course. An insulated cool-box is desirable.

Buy the essentials early; the shops will shut at noon or 12.30 p.m. (More on shops and shopping in Chapter 14.) Immediately after breakfast is a good time, if you are staying in a hotel in a town; otherwise, at the first shops you come across. A loaf of bread is what we chiefly need. Choose a *boulangerie* by the appetising smell of hot loaves coming out of the oven. Do you really need butter? Perhaps in Normandy, where it is delicious, if the weather is cool; otherwise, reflect on the animal fats that will be in what you are next going to buy. Choose a *charcuterie* and/or a *rôtisserie* by the window display and the number of people waiting to be served: the more the merrier, because this isn't preserved factory food – fast turnover and popularity are virtues, and worth waiting ten minutes for. Besides, one sees what is being bought: no two *charcuteries* are the same, and a little observation pays dividends. What will there be? See the sections on *la charcuterie* and *la rôtisserie*, and having bought basics like ham or pâté, always try something new – but do remember to say *c'est pour un piquenique*, and then you won't find you have got something that needs cooking or at least warming gently (some pies – *pâtés en croûte* – need warming, others definitely not). Eggs in jelly, with decorations? Ready-mixed salads? *Crudités*, such as ready-seasoned grated carrot or celeriac? A helping of paella? A hot roast chicken? (that might be at *la boucherie*, though).

Wine, beer, mineral water, Coca-Cola – at the *épicerie*, perhaps from a refrigerated section. Pudding? There's the *pâtisserie*, but take good care of its wares: they are fragile and probably need keeping the right way up. Fruit? There should be lots.

You have now laid the foundation. If, however, you are a *gourmet* or a *gourmand* (*gourmets* are OK, *gourmands* are greedy), you will hope to meet more temptations *en route*. Sold by the roadside, are cherries in the spring and peaches in the summer, in the districts where they grow. Perhaps you will pass another *charcuterie* with hitherto undiscovered specimens in the window.

Sophie and I have gone native. We are *sérieux* about picnics. We take a folding table and chairs, and real wineglasses. A cool white wine doesn't taste the same out of a plastic mug, and we need white wine if we are going to pass the place where we buy the oysters. (The man gives us the lemon, free.)

Don't build a twig fire in a forest to do a little grilling! There are probably great big notices telling one not to. Thousands and thousands of acres go up in smoke every tourist season, and the locals don't like it. (While on the subject, it is all right to throw lighted cigarette ends out of the car window in England's green and pleasantly damp land, but *not* in the Midi in August.)

The above sounds very elaborate. Good simple snacking can be done on a park bench in the middle of a town, if one buys the food before twelve. Some cafés (not the poshest sort) don't mind if one picnics at their table, so long as one drinks their drinks. Best to ask, if you don't see other people doing it with the apparent blessing of the management: *est-ce que je peux piqueniquer?* The custom is dying out, though, as so many cafés sell *le croque-monsieur* and even *le hot-dog*; much less recommendable than a personally bought picnic.

Bon appétit!

Chapter 11

Camping and caravanning

The French National Tourist Office issues camping leaflets (large stamped addressed envelope, please).

For campsites, the green Michelin Camping and Caravanning guide does what the red Michelin guide does for hotels and restaurants: it gives a selection of sites (a wide one), with succinct details, mostly in symbol form with a multilingual explanation. Summer campers in the south will learn to look for the symbol that means shade if they hope to include a siesta in their routine (advisable: camping always fills me with joy and energy at dawn and gives me a brisk appetite at midday but slumber takes over soon after). The guide also shows which sites accept caravans and whether power points are available.

There are great numbers of big campsites on the coast, but these are crowded in July and August. Inland, there is usually plenty of room; one can still sunbathe, and the Michelin guide shows which sites are by lakes or rivers suitable for swimming.

Campsites, like hotels, are officially graded, with a star system. Grade and prices are exhibited outside. Luxurious ones (hot showers, swimming pool, ample marked-out *emplacements* for each tent) could cost as much as 100 francs per day for a family of four in 1985. These are too much like small towns for some people, especially when – as on the Mediterranean coast – they are full.

Campers can be divided into stayers and nomads. Some French stayers go every year for a month to the same campsite, taking elaborate equipment and the family cat on a lead; I have seen some who manage to raise a row of radishes. Nomads need simpler quarters. Sophie and I and our children had never camped in our lives before venturing the experience in France; for people who prefer to spend a maximum of three nights in any one place we lumbered ourselves with too luxurious a tent. The first time we erected it, it took over an hour. We finally got it down to twenty minutes, with a rigorous delegation of responsibilities. Unless the reader intends to be a stayer, I advise the simplest tent that will cover the party. One does really need a folding table and light chairs, though, and some part of the tent should extend to shade them: camp food in France can be delightful – see the chapter on picnics (page 95) – and one should be able to enjoy it in comfort. An insulated cool box, with a couple of those thermal packs that one can freeze if the campsite facilities permit, is almost essential; one doesn't want *warm* white wine. The simplest one-burner Camping-Gaz cooker is enough. We found a pressure-cooker worth taking; not just for pressure-cooking, but because the lid gets firmly fixed, minimising danger if it gets knocked over; it also makes a good 'hay-box' cooker for stews, if one wraps a sleeping bag around it and leaves it for an afternoon, and it is a good place for storing things that spill (opened bags of sugar, etc.) when on the move.

It is possible to experiment with camping by booking a holiday with a firm that provides ready-erected luxury tents, with fridge and all. These are usually on big popular sites on the coast, with ice-cream parlours and candy-floss booths lining the path to the beach; a different experience from exploring lesser-known parts of France according to whim and weather, communing with nature, fishing in mountain streams and buying one's provisions from farms and country markets. In the long run we found that what suited us best was to use the simplest campsites, and once a week have a night in a hotel.

One needs a *Camping Carnet*, to hand in at the campsite office; obtainable from motoring organisations, etc. This shows that one has third-party cover in case one causes damage, and is a proof of respectability.

Chapter 12

Holiday villas; gîtes

There is a lot to be said for a lazy spell in a hotel, letting someone else make the beds, do the shopping and cook the meals. But in recent years more and more British holiday-makers have taken to do-it-yourself holidays in France. This can save money, especially for families, and many people prefer self-catering anyway. When in hotels they may have felt frustrated as they wandered round markets and gazed into shop windows, wishing they had a cooking-stove and their copies of Elizabeth David and Jane Grigson. Or passing through some pleasant village they may have felt how interesting it would be to try to integrate themselves, in a small way, learning what goes on at the farm, discovering how the locals live and joining in some of the village activities.

There are half a dozen *gîtes* in the village Sophie and I live in, and from time to time British people rent them. Some just use the place for an inexpensive holiday, driving off every day to the beach (40 minutes) or the lake (10 minutes), lunching at a restaurant somewhere, buying simple rations at a super-market, and using their *gîte* only for supper, sleep and breakfast. They are usually well satisfied, especially with the independence this sort of holiday allows. Others go for rambles in the hills, make friends with villagers, play *pétanque*, learn about how a vineyard works and even give a hand sometimes, and buy their provisions from the travelling grocer and butcher who halt in the square twice a week, letting the village ladies tell them what they ought to buy and satisfying the curiosity of the locals . . . they 'go native' for a fortnight, as far as they can, and if they have small children it helps wonderfully (the French are suckers for small children). It has been done on about ten words of French, cheerful smiles and a willingness to have a go. Such people are usually full of enthusiasm; many first-timers declare they have had the holiday of their lives, and come back again or do the same sort of thing in another part of France.

I must say I am grateful to both types. This book should be dedicated to them. It owes much to their questions, remarks and tales of adventure (and a certain amount to villagers' confidential comments on these exotic visitors. . . . I am glad to be able to report that most British *gîte*-dwellers earn high marks for being *gentils* and *sympathiques*, i.e. nice, especially in comparison with some other 'foreigners', including Parisians).

France must be the easiest country in the world for renting self-catering accommodation, whether in towns, at seaside resorts or in rural areas. The free *Traveller in France*, issued by the French National Tourist Office, lists a couple of hundred agencies with British offices, and for big towns and seaside resorts it would be best to start from there. But when it comes to country districts, I am going to sing the praises of the Gîtes de France organisation.

A *gîte rural* is a holiday villa, or flat, or self-contained part of a house, with its own lockable front door, bathroom with at least a shower and a basin, a sit-down flushing loo, a fridge, adequate cooking facilities and utensils, and decent if simple furniture and equipment for living (except sheets and towels – these can sometimes be hired at extra cost); it is under the umbrella of the Fédération Nationale des Gîtes de France, and has been inspected, graded and listed by departmental officials and had its rent approved as reasonable for its grade and size. It must then exhibit the round green *Gîte de France* plaque outside. It is usually very good value. French people do not like selling off house property (it is regarded as an inflation-proof investment); they may get favourable loans or tax concessions if they convert a cottage into a *gîte* of the approved standard and guarantee to let it for holiday use for a number of years, because the authorities want to encourage rural areas in this way.

From now on I shall use the word *gîte* to mean an 'official' *gîte* of this sort. (Its dictionary meaning is any kind of lodging or home, including a hare's form.)

The snag about *gîtes* is that in July and August the French are in them. French workers have five weeks' paid holiday a year. Papa will probably take a week or two in the winter, for ski-ing, or at Easter, but Maman and the children may take a *gîte* for six weeks, leaving Papa to come down for his remaining three. They booked the *gîte* the previous summer. Outside July and August the position is different, and I shall deal with it later.

The first-timer who wants a *gîte* in the high season and can deal with the matter early in the year is strongly advised to contact the London office: Gîtes de France, 178 Piccadilly, W1V 0AL – the same address as the French National Tourist Office. They issue, very early in the year or even before Christmas, a thick booklet containing a lot of useful information and a descriptive list, with photographs, of nearly 2000 *gîtes* that are reserved for British bookings until some time in the spring. Booking, including reduced-rate car-ferry and insurance, can be done through the London office. You have to be a member; this costs something like £3. The first step is to send the London office a stamped addressed envelope for details.

If, however, you want something at a seaside resort, or in a town, or with a private swimming pool and luxurious interior decoration, you should apply to an agency. *Gîtes* (that is, *gîtes ruraux*, alias Gîtes de France) are in the country, in villages or on farms, and – with exceptions – fairly simple.

Although the London Gîtes de France office covers a lot of *gîtes*, they are only a selection. There are thousands more. Each *département* ('county') issues its departmental list. For example, the *département* of the Ardèche is almost exactly one hundredth the size of France, and it has over 1000 *gîtes* in its booklet. A list of a *département's gîtes* can usually be obtained by writing to the Office du Tourisme or Syndicat d'Initiative in the county town; one way of finding its address is by looking in the Guide Michelin (in the public library, if it's too early for the current year's edition to have appeared) where county towns are indicated by a P (for préfecture) after the name of the town, and Tourist Office addresses below that. Please enclose an International Reply Coupon. You may be able to make your booking through the local Office du Tourisme, or you may have to deal with the owner of the *gîte* direct.

Agencies listed in the French National Tourist Office's leaflet deal with 'official' *gîtes* as well as other properties, sometimes charging more than the normal *gîte* rent; such agencies earn their money by providing extra information in English and sometimes extra services.

Outside July and August the situation is different. France is your oyster, *gîte*-wise. First-timers, and people who like to have everything organised well in advance, should no doubt book as above. But if one prefers to play it by ear, taking it easy and looking around, and if one has a few extra days in which to do so, one could arrive in the area of one's choice, stay at a hotel for a night or two and expect to find a suitable *gîte*. One profits from the rigidity of French habits with summer holiday dates. Efforts to stagger French school holidays are vigorously resisted. The Frenchman who takes his summer break before I July or after 31 August is a rare bird. The luckiest people are those who can idle in France in April, May, June, September, October in the south, and even November in good years. *Gîtes* galore, and much cheaper too.

One can call at a Syndicat d'Initiative or an Office du

Tourisme, in a town with pleasing surroundings. They might fix one up straight away, or provide a list so that one can have a look at several places. Or if one comes across a village that takes one's fancy, and there's no Syndicat d'Initiative, see if the *mairie* (town hall) is open. (In our village, population 80, the *mairie* is open from 6.30 p.m. to 8 p.m., give or take half an hour either way.) A *mairie* is a Registry of Births, Marriages and Deaths, a Passport Office, a Citizen's Advice Bureau, the local Land Registry, the Parish Council HQ and a lot more. (French mayors are different from British ones: they are salaried part-time officials, elected for six years.) Anyway, at the *mairie* they know all about it, and will usually be delighted to help. Some *gîtes* may in fact belong to the *commune* (a *gîte communal* has nothing to do with communal living: the rent helps to keep the rates down).

Or a mention at a village café: '*Je voudrais trouver un gîte rural*' may set wheels in motion. The same can even go for old ladies sitting in the shade in the square.

But for a *gîte* in a biggish town or a seaside resort, the Syndicat d'Initiative is the best place to go. Estate agents (*agents immobiliers*) have short-let accommodation on their books, but not *gîtes ruraux* as such. *Un meublé* (short for *un appartement meublé*, a furnished apartment) means any sort of furnished accommodation for letting.

What to expect from your gîte rural

Cooking will probably be on bottled gas (*le gaz* – Butagaz, Propagaz, etc.) and it will perhaps work the water-heater too (*le chauffe-eau*). A cylinder (*le cylindre,* or *la bouteille*) is a heavy affair, and you should certainly get your landlord to change it himself. It takes only a couple of minutes, but one needs to know how. He will want to anyway, for fear of strange people wrecking the property. A cylinder contains 13kg of liquid gas; for cooking, it lasts the average family of four about six weeks, but if it works the *chauffe-eau* it will run out much quicker. Make sure that you get the *chauffe-eau* explained – it is only a matter of a tap or two – and how to get the pilot light (*la veilleuse*) going. There is a master tap on the top of the gas cylinder, and they do like you to turn that off when you go out for the day – which of course puts the pilot light out. Don't worry if your French is rudimentary – it's all done by gestures and action.

Heating is usually an extra. It may well be that you have *un poêle à mazout* – a stove that works on fuel oil. You pour in a few litres of *mazout*, but it is *not* like a paraffin stove (the Aladdin or Valor kind). It has a chimney going outside, and there is a special technique for lighting it, and another one for turning it off. Do make sure that these have been clearly explained, and do rehearse under your instructor's eyes. Both operations are child's play, but French country-dwellers are so used to such *poêles* that they do not realise they are a novelty to most Britons. Turning off is most important: if you leave the drip feed going, when you come home and try to light up you may get a God-awful cloud of black smoke from the *poêle* and cries of alarm and despondency from all around.

As for the furniture, official *gîtes ruraux* are classified in three grades for comfort, and priced accordingly. But even in the top grade there may be a lack of comfortable deep easy chairs. The traditional French habit (changing now) was to spend free time in the evening around the dining table, sitting on ordinary chairs. Your landlord may have bought himself the familiar British-style three-piece suite for telly-watching, but he will not have thought such items essential for what he considers as a place for summer letting. There might be – especially in a *gîte* with a bit of garden or private open space – decent collapsible open-air chairs. If you have sabbatical leave and are going to spend the winter in a *gîte* in the south of France, your landlord should give you the red carpet treatment, so if he can't provide an armchair (*le fauteuil*) and proper *lampes* for reading by, don't take his *gîte*.

If you sit around indoors in warm summer nights with the windows open and the lights on, of course insects will fly in, and you will be buying aerosols (*une bombe*!; people who spray graffiti are *bombagistes*) of *insecticide* at the *droguerie*; only lucky tenants find fly-screens at the windows. This brings us to hot-weather drill, and shutters.

The first thing that French children say when they come to England is *Quoi? Pas de volets?* – 'What, no shutters?'. In France, windows open inwards, and shutters open outwards. (They also, it is hoped, keep burglars out. The locals will be surprised if you go out for the day, and especially a day and a night, leaving your shutters open.) The shutters take the place of heavy curtains, so normally they would be shut at night, leaving cooling air to come in through the interstices and the open windows.

When it's hot in the daytime – say 90°F in the shade – windows are open but shutters are shut, to keep the sun from heating the tiled floor. If the daytime air is even hotter, the windows are shut too. People like to come in and say 'Aah! Nice and cool!' However, it is well known that Britons in the Midi like to be too hot.

Now for a point of etiquette, or considerate behaviour. It's a free country, and if in high summer Britons like to sleep through the delicious early-morning hours and then go and play beach cricket at midday in the glare of a Mediterranean shore, good luck to them. But if you have a *gîte* in a country village in the south where your neighbours are engaged in agricultural pursuits, they will have been up at five so as to get half the day's work or more done by eleven. Twelve to two will be their 'lunch hour', when they have their main meal of the day, followed by a siesta. Beard them in their dens at 12 noon (*téléphonez HR* say the small ads – phone at *heures des repas* – meal-times) but try to respect their afternoon sleep. They need it; they will start work again at (British) tea-time, and carry on until late; a light supper, a little chat or *pétanque* (steel bowls on gravel, under the street light or at the village *boulodrome*) in the cool, and then bed at 11 or 12 p.m. Now the French are great respecters of privacy, and tolerant of noise and other nuisances *until something snaps*. In campsites, the rule of silence after about 10.30 p.m. is usually well observed; but there was once a family of highly respectable Britons in a *gîte* in our village who liked to take late suppers in the moonlight on their terrace, right under the windows of a hard-working wine-grower (you need to spray vines around dawn). Lots of nice cool white wine, and shrieks of happy laughter until one or two in the morning. . . . Then bed until nine or ten. I imagine that in England, if a party just outside had been whooping it up in a foreign tongue for some four hours before getting-up time, someone would have come down the first night and said 'Would you mind, dear people . . .' – but here, it wasn't until the fifth morning that the lady of the house exploded; and to me, rather than to the family in question. (It is one of the drawbacks of being the local Englishman: one is taken to be responsible for the doings of one's compatriots: Mrs Thatcher, Mr Scargill, HM the Queen and football supporters.) All was smoothed over, and harmony restored. But one often wishes that the southern French were not so tolerant of noise for so long, and if you have a travelling funfair establishing itself within ear-shot you might regret that the theoretical rule about *tapage nocturne* (nocturnal din-making) after 10.30 p.m. is totally suspended while the *fête* lasts.

As I said, you will probably be cooking on gas. There will be gas-rings and no doubt an oven, but probably no grill. There might be a barbecue (*un barbecue*) outside, and if you are among the vineyards your landlord might be able to produce some of the winter's vine-prunings (*des sarments de vigne*) to burn for grilling (*pour griller*). Down in the Midi people are rightly afraid of setting fire to the surrounding vegetation, so if you have brought a camping barbecue, do ask where it would be thought safe to use it. Fresh sardines, *sardines fraîches*, if you are near a sardine-landing port and if you can get them really bright-eyed and fresh, are delicious (grill them just as they are: the skin lifts off easily when you eat them barbarically in the fingers, sucking the flesh off the bones and leaving the guts). They are best cooked outside. They spurt and hiss, creating steam and smoke; the smell is lovely when you're hungry but you don't want it hanging around for the next twelve hours.

For inside cooking without a grill, sautéing is a good French way of cooking, for example, steak. Put a smear of cooking oil into the frying-pan and sauté the steak until it is done to your taste; pour a couple of tablespoons of table wine into the pan. As it boils, scrape up all the baked-on juices, and when most of the meaty winey liquid has evaporated, pour the remaining reduction over the steak. (This basic French procedure is called *déglaçage*.) A little softened butter can be swirled into the *jus*.

There might be what is called *un gril*, or *une plaque à griller*, among the equipment. This is a flat round black cast iron or steel affair, with a folding metal handle. It has deep ridges on its cooking surface, about half an inch apart. You heat it on the gas ring, and fling the steak onto the ridges, which leave nice parallel burnt lines. Some people become fond of such *grils*, and buy one to take home – they are quite cheap.

Things to bring

- Sheets and towels (*le drap, la serviette*). These can often be hired, at an extra charge, but not always (if necessary, enquire in advance).

- A teapot (*la théière*) if you can't do without one. The average French person drinks tea only when very ill. If your *gîte* has had a long line of British tenants, all of whom have asked *Où est la théière?*, a pot might have been bought as a friendly gesture. Tea can be made in a saucepan, though. There will naturally be adequate coffee-making equipment, perhaps even a coffee-grinder, as they drink instant coffee only in emergencies (or on trains, and how they grumble).

- Tea (*le thé*). Tea-leaves, unreliably rumoured to have been recycled from the bottoms of teapots in Whitehall, HM prisons and NHS hospitals and exported to France, are on sale at a shocking price. Coffee is cheaper and better than in Britain. It pays to go native, and Sophie and I have coffee for breakfast; however, one can't make breakfast without getting up first, and it's hard to get up without tea.

Theoretically, the French Customs allow only 150g, about five ounces, per head, but we always bring three or four pounds back from visits to England, and our friends and relations are firmly instructed to do the same if they want a warm welcome. The French Customs have more important things to bother about, it seems, and have no Typhoo-sniffing dogs.

- Your favourite instant coffee (usually called *le nescafé*) if you really can't bear to make proper coffee. Instant coffee can be found at supermarkets, but it may take a number of experimental purchases to find a sort you like.

- Your favourite cook's knife, if you are a real Foodie. Unlikely that a costly carbon-steel *couteau du chef* will be left at the mercy of a string of tenants.

- I have heard complaints that some *gîtes* lack eggcups (*le coquetier*, so called because a boiled egg is *un oeuf à la coque*, i.e. in the shell). The French don't usually have boiled eggs for breakfast, and eggs turn up in other shapes at other meals.

- Particular addictions, such as Marmite, peanut butter and pickles, may be found only with great difficulty. Tomato ketchup is on sale, and Worcester Sauce sometimes (the French call it *sauce anglaise*; it says Worcester on the bottle but only advanced students can pronounce that), but not other British-type bottled sauces. The French like to think of themselves as having two carefully cooked meals a day, tasting of what they are made of, and claim that the British get bland tasteless dishes onto which they slosh harsh violent bottled flavours. Slander! So keep the incriminating evidence out of sight, and twit the French with the rash of Macdonalds that has recently sprung up.

- Heinz Baked Beans. Not for you, of course: you are in the land of plenty and opportunity, but for children with old-fashioned ideas about messed-up foreign muck, who can be made happy by such economical and trouble-free fodder. Tins of *haricots à la sauce tomate* are not quite the same; less sugar. If you can fob the brats off with

111

Instant Mash, there's some in the supermarket (*purée de pommes de terre en flocons*).

That is about all for the store cupboard. Many first-timers overdo it. I have even seen them unloading potatoes, which are better in France. One look round a decent French market cures all that. However, Sophie insists that I put in a plug for mild green Fairy Liquid, which she says is better than any *liquide pour vaisselle* (*faire la vaisselle* means to do the washing up) she has yet found in France. Don't think I never *faire la vaisselle*, but I'm not a connoisseur. She also says bring a candle (*une bougie*). Why? Because down in the Midi, in high summer, we sometimes have a real Mediterranean thunderstorm and the electricity goes off for an hour or two, and she's always lending candles to people in the *gîte*. Of course candles can be bought, but not at 10 p.m. while the thunder rattles around the hills.

Oh, yes – whisky (*le whisky*). It's about 20 per cent cheaper on the boat than in France. The French think whisky is *très chic*, and if you are in a *gîte* you will probably get presents of wine, fruit and vegetables; the offer of *un petit Scotch* is an acceptable and appropriate return. French singles are British doubles.

Additional gîte *vocabulary*

la location – renting, hiring (*Location de voitures*: car hire)
le locataire – the tenant, the hirer
louer – to rent, to hire
le propriétaire – the owner, the landlord
la réservation, réserver – booking, to book
les arrhes (pronounced *ar*, with some sort of R sound – Parisian uvular or Scottish-Perpignan trilled) – the deposit as part payment of rent; sometimes *les arrhes* are called *un à valoir*. *Une caution* is a refundable deposit against possible damage.
l'inventaire (m.) – inventory

les dégats – damage to things

l'indemnisation (f.) – compensation for damage (i.e. 'damages' in the financial sense)

le loyer – the rent

la cuisinière – the cooking-stove (and the female cook)

le débouchoir – the rubber plunger, for when *l'évier* (the sink) gets bunged up

l'oreiller – the pillow. There probably won't be one, as *un traversin* (a bolster) is the normal thing. But you might get one if you ask. Some difficult sleepers bring their own.

la poubelle – the dustbin, for *les ordures,* the rubbish

le courrier – the mail, letters. (*Voudriez-vous faire suivre mon courrier?* 'Will you please forward my mail?')

Chapter 13

Fishing

Angling (*la pêche à la ligne*) is a popular activity. Well-stocked shops selling *articles de pêche* abound wherever there are good rivers and lakes and/or hopeful fishermen. Such shops issue fishing licences (*le permis de pêche*), the proceeds of which are devoted to *la pisciculture*, the encouragement of fish to be fruitful and multiply. One should not fish without a licence; the police can ask to see it. The cost is small – fishing is a proletarian pastime. The small print on the licence gives the local regulations, and the man in the tackle shop will give good advice.

Rivers are divided into two categories. In *la première catégorie* trout and salmon predominate, and maggots (*des asticots*, m.) are banned; in *la deuxième catégorie* almost anything goes except fish-eggs. The close season is different for the two categories, though even then Sunday fishing may be allowed. Details from the fishing-tackle shop. If one is going to be in a place for only a week or two, advice will be forthcoming about what sort of licence to get. A distinction may be made between *la pêche au coup*, where one puts down ground-bait (and where the French usually fish without a reel: just a long rod with a line of the same length tied to the end) and *la pêche au lancer*, which involves casting and spinning, or using live bait.

The Michelin Camping and Caravanning guide shows which campsites have fishing nearby. I knew one where I could fish in pyjamas, just outside the tent, at dawn in summer, and rely on landing a couple of trout for breakfast . . . Well, not exactly rely, and sometimes they were only chub. . . .

Chapter 14

Le Shopping

It has been suggested that this book should contain a list of bargains to bring home from France. I refuse. You, gentle but independent-minded reader, can spot a bargain when you see one, and you know whether you want it or not. Anyway, in our complicated world, lists of 'best buys' go out of date rapidly, as a result of changes in taxation, new internal or Common Market regulations encouraging or forbidding competition, a country's treaties with its ex-colonies and other factors that have nothing to do with traditional skills or the climate. And then there are fluctuations in the rate of exchange. In the mid-seventies, at eight francs to the pound, French families were taking day trips from Calais and Boulogne and coming back chortling with legs of lamb, woollies and pots and pans, plus the suitcase full of washing that Grandmère had done at the Dover washeteria. In the mid-eighties, at twelve francs to the pound, the boot was on the other foot: not only booze and cast-iron ovenware – one keen Englishman was seen wheeling a small electric cement mixer on board the boat.

Apart from the ration of alcoholic drinks and tobacco products, at the time of writing one could bring back miscellaneous things up to the value of £120, but not chrysanthemums, pork, poultry, offal or trees; you could include five plants or parts of plants. When does a large plant become a small tree? Well, bargain-hunters must check with the Customs as they leave England, and if they enjoy themselves in the shops I hope they won't find out later that they could have saved 50p by going to Marks & Spencer. I am a sucker for ironmongers, and when I lived in England I had a collection of items that could only be bought in France, including a three-hole mouse-trap for one bright mouse, one stupid mouse and one proper Charlie. We never used it, and Sophie said that I was the proper Charlie. I found it of great sentimental value, though.

One difference, mainly with manufactured goods, is that in France there is a greater spread of prices for the same item from shop to shop. Keen shoppers will look around before buying. I am all for patronising small shops for fresh food, but a household gadget or a shirt made in the Far East can cost 50 per cent more in a small-town High-Street shop than in a hypermarket, and 30 per cent more in one hypermarket than in another, while the dearer hypermarket will be cheaper for something else. Last Christmas a survey in Montpellier showed a price difference of 77 per cent for a standard Monopoly set (they play it in France) and 141 per cent (the record) for a certain German-made toy. Toys at Christmas are extreme examples, but watch the careful French housewife in the marketplace, going the rounds, comparing price and quality.

On the other hand, price differences can reflect differences in quality, above all with food. The French are somewhat wealthier than the British, on average, and they are willing to spend a greater proportion of their income on food. In the small market town near where I live, the best chickens cost three times as much as the cheapest. Alas for Britain, the cheapest are better than the usual British bird. The dearest are free range and have been fed on maize: a totally different proposition from our familiar watery swindle, raised too quickly on fishy abominations and killed too young. Perhaps the Briton is reluctant to fork out for a proper 'pre-war'-type chicken (in those far-off pre-battery days chicken was a luxury, unlike roast beef), or perhaps British suppliers hold that 'there's no demand for it.' There are signs that the demand is shouting loud enough to be heard – after all, decent bread can once again be found here and there in the British Isles. No rich people live in our nearest little town, it isn't in a fashionable area, but in addition to selling everyday provisions the shops and market stalls do a fair trade in items of a kind and quality that, in London, one might hope to find only in Harrods Food Halls or somewhere similar.

It would be misleading to give the impression that the self-caterer needs to spend more than in Britain on the housekeeping. True, he can, and if he shops carefully he will get good luxury value. But the holiday-maker with more time than money can stretch his francs without being reduced to poor quality provisions, and camp for four or five weeks on a budget that would last his more easily tempted neighbour only a fortnight. With sun and shade and swimming a diet of bread, wine, cheese and fruit, and a little steak on Sundays, is no hardship.

Tactics

One mustn't be snooty about monster hypermarkets. (Hyper-markets are officially defined as supermarkets with over 2500 square metres of selling space – well over half an acre.) Museums and art galleries are all very well in their own way, but a visit to an exotic *hypermarché* is great fun, and one is encouraged to put the exhibits in one's trolley (*le chariot*). Auchan, Carrefour, Casino, Euromarché, Intermarché, Mammouth, Montlaur and others, with their big car parks, on the outskirts of towns, may not offer much in the way of human relationships, but – like, at the other extreme, the typical street market – they are worth a visit even if one isn't going to buy anything.

Clustered around the *hypermarché* there may be a *centre commercial*: an arcade with little shops – a newsagent, hairdressers, souvenirs, expensive clothes, sweets . . . petrol pumps, perhaps a garden centre, a café or a cafeteria; toilets and washing facilities, phone booths, booths for the instant portrait photographs that the French need so often . . .

Inside the *hypermarché* itself there will be television sets and microwave ovens, clothes, clocks, cheap make-up, books, cassettes and records, three-piece suites (free loan of self-drive van for an hour to take them away in, sometimes) and an enormous range of food and drink. Not just packets and tins and deep-frozen things, but a stupendous array of fresh fish including live lobsters; fruit and vegetables; meat and game; delicatessen foods . . . Only the less interesting of these fresh items will be pre-packed, because the French housewife does not like to buy her food that way. She picks out the fruit and vegetables she wants and puts them into plastic bags, and queues to have them weighed and labelled with the price. Similarly she likes to get close to her fish, without a cellophane barrier between nose and smell; and she wants the butcher to cut her steak to her instructions. All this means queueing three or four times before one reaches the check-out queue, and I find the process pure hell, especially as I don't much care for the moronic piped music that slops out from the loudspeakers. Sophie finds it convenient to take me to one every six weeks or so. If it were once a year I would love it.

If one is self-catering in a *gîte* or under canvas, an early trip round a *hypermarché* is a good idea. Basic factory-packed stores can be laid in, a little more cheaply than at the village shop. Treat the place as a museum and get a good idea of the cost of a wide range of items. Having done this bit of shopping by *chariot* and car, one can shop during the rest of one's stay like a civilised human being, with a shopping basket.

Notes on the goods on sale in the *hypermarché* will be found under the headings for various shops, below. See also 'Wine'

119

(page 173) and 'Beer' (page 191).

Real shops are different. Of course, in a Parisian shop in the rush hour it is sensible to make up one's mind as to what one wants and to avoid dithering like a benighted provincial. But when one is in the blessedly benighted provinces, and above all in small family-run shops near where one is staying, one may find a different conception of efficiency. Many small shops have gone out of business in the last twenty years because of the competition from *hypermarchés* and *supermarchés* and the universal spread of the motorcar, but there are still many more small shops than in Britain, and more than an efficiency expert would prescribe. The competition between them seems based on the individuality of the goods on offer (especially among the bakers) and on the service given; each shop has its faithful customers, and the shopkeeper takes a personal interest in them, by no means insincere as far as I can judge. Most of the small shopkeepers I know seem happy in their work despite the long hours they put in; they enjoy human relationships at an admittedly superficial level. (The travelling grocer who comes to my village on Tuesdays and Saturdays knows everybody by name, carries news and messages from village to village and does a 75–80-hour week; then, three evenings a week, he plays his trumpet at the local brass band rehearsals, and on two more evenings coaches a junior rugby team. The life seems to suit him. In 1980 I wrote a piece about him for a Parisian paper. As a result a German TV team came and spent a week filming his activities. Oh, how he loved it! He is a very extravert character.)

Shops catering exclusively for tourists (for example, groceries serving big campsites) are, predictably, another matter. Apart from those, if you are shopping in the high season and if no more than a quarter of the customers are summer visitors and other 'foreigners', the question in the minds of the shopkeeper and the regulars is: are you a human being? If you are, you will have said *bonjour, messieurs-dames* to the assembled company as you enter, and you will appear to take a deep interest in the goings-on. You will not be in a hurry; having waited patiently while the old lady in front buys *one* little slice of ham and *one* little slice of pâté – which of the six sorts of pâté? Ah, that will take a few minutes ... there's X who doesn't like garlic (*il ne supporte pas l'ail*) and there's Y who is on a salt-free diet (*un régime sans sel*), and Z who is just *difficile* – and umpteen other bits and pieces, you would think that those who came in after you would be delighted if you were quick off the mark. But no: that would show no respect for the stuff on sale. They want you to take it seriously. Ask; explain what you want it for; let them savour your accent and satisfy some of their curiosity (Oh, so you haven't got a grill at Mr So-and-so's *gîte*? Well, you'd better have this rather than that, it does nicely in a frying-pan ... oh, if you're going on a picnic don't have that sort of pie, it needs warming up for its full beauty to be appreciated ... um, yes, our andouillettes are home-made but I always thought the English didn't like andouillettes – you *are* English, aren't you?). By this time everyone is reassured about you. *Au revoir, messieurs-dames.* You will be discussed. Next time, you will be known. Madame shopkeeper will have remembered what you bought, she hopes you remember too and would like to hear your reactions. Don't refuse free samples! Shopping, especially for food, is a serious (*sérieux* – not gloomy, but responsible) business. Three or four visits like that, and there is a fifty-fifty chance that you will be remembered next year.

The old-fashioned French housewife's ideal would be to go food-shopping twice a day. (Working women and their husbands load up the *chariot* at the supermarket weekly; a different way of life.) So one slice of ham, or two little sausages, or three thin slices of *saucisson sec*, is a perfectly acceptable small-shop order. One carrot, one leek, one onion? But of course! That's how cooking is done. An Englishwoman once told me 'I couldn't buy any lettuce because the price was marked per kilo, and I didn't want over two pounds ...' It was sold by weight because the lettuce were local, and of different sizes; she should have rummaged delicately among them to find the one she wanted, and it would have been weighed.

I have never yet been short-changed in France, though attempts have been made (in the tourist belt); usually by giving me the wrong note (at present there is a 20-franc note that looks vaguely like a 100-franc note) or by apparent forgetfulness of the fact that I had proffered a 200-franc note rather than a 100-franc one. Effusive apologies. But when one is on the human-being level, if it is thought that one is unfamiliar with the currency, expressive slow-motion counting will be indulged in, and one can have confidence. There was an American lady who stayed in a *gîte* in my village. One Wednesday she went to the weekly market, four miles away, and managed somehow to leave a bag containing money, passport, American Express card, etc., on one of the market stalls; she didn't notice that it wasn't in her shopping basket till she got home ... She was about to send off telegrams to all and sundry, when the police phoned me up: 'Is there an American lady in your village? A stall holder has brought in a bag and it looks quite valuable. . . .' Of course this is rather a backward area. Thank heaven there are a lot of backward areas in France, and long may they remain so. In Marseilles and in some Paris *métro* stations, keep handbags firmly pressed to the body. (You see, I have become a benighted provincial: when I am in Paris I keep my wits about me ... and then I find a corner shop or café that is just like the deep south.)

For shop opening times see page 19.

Weights and measures/ Shopping vocabulary

Weights: 1kg, *un kilo*, is 2.2 lb. 500g, *cinq cent grammes*, is usually called *une livre* (feminine, unlike *un livre* – a book) and is a good pound. (£1 is *une livre sterling*.) 100g, *cent grammes*, is a scant quarter pound. Occasionally labelled *un hecto*, short for *un hectogramme*.

Volume: 1 *litre* (m.), now known on both sides of the Channel, is 1¾ British pints or an American quart. Usually broken down into *millilitres* (ml). A 500ml bottle of olive oil is a scant British pint.

Une tranche de —— – a slice of —— A thin slice – *une tranche mince;* a fairly thick slice – *une tranche pas trop mince.* (In the Midi, for food, *joli,* pretty, is often used to mean big; *une jolie tranche de jambon* would be called, in Cornwall, a proper handsome slice of ham. *Un joli poulet* is a chicken weighing over 2kg.)

La moitié de ——, *un demi-* —— – half of ——, a half-——

Un petit bout de —— – *a small chunk of* —— *(cheese, salami, etc.).*

Pour une personne, pour deux personnes – enough for one, for two. Typically, a ration of take-away food *pour deux personnes* will give three or more average British servings. If not enough: *encore un petit peu* – a bit more. *Assez! Ça va comme ça!* That's enough! *C'est trop!* Too much!

Je peux me servir? – Do I help myself? (Sometimes you do: with ordinary fruit and vegetables, for example, and at some bakers.)

C'est pour offrir? You might be asked this when buying, for example, expensive confectionery. *Offrir* means 'to give as a present', so the question means 'Would you like it gift-wrapped?' Usually beautifully done, and at no extra charge. If you want books, scent, etc., gift-wrapped, say *C'est pour offrir.*

Prices are supposed to be clearly shown, and usually are. It may not always be clear, with objects like pineapples, whether the price is per kilo or apiece. *C'est dix francs le kilo? C'est dix francs la pièce?*

With loose small items like olives and nuts, one might ask for 10 francs' worth: *pour dix francs d'olives.*

Old and new francs: see remarks about numbers on page 201. You are unlikely nowadays to hear *dix francs* referred to as *mille francs,* but F2,50 might be called *deux cent cinquante* (francs) instead of *deux francs cinquante* – in the market, especially with a stall-holder who is used to dealing with conservative-minded old ladies who persist in calling centimes francs.

Individual shops are described under their French names:

baker – *la boulangerie* (page 130)
bank – *la banque* (see below)
bookshop – *la librairie* (page 146)
butcher – *la boucherie, la charcuterie* (pages 126 and 132)
cake shop, pastrycook – *la pâtisserie* (page 146)
chemist – *la pharmacie* (page 147)
dairy products – *la crémerie* (page 136)
delicatessen – *la charcuterie* (page 132)
dry cleaning – strictly, *la teinturerie* or *le nettoyage à sec*, but dealt with here under *la blanchisserie* (page 125)
fishmonger – *la poissonnerie* (page 149)
greengrocer – *fruits et légumes* (page 143)
grocery – *l'épicerie* (page 138)
haberdashery – *la mercerie* (page 146)
hairdresser – *coiffure* (page 134)
ironmongery – see *la droguerie* and *la quincaillerie* (pages 137 and 155)
laundry – *la blanchisserie* (page 125)
market – see *fruits et légumes* (page 143)
post office – *le bureau de poste* (PTT) (page 154)
sweet shop – *la confiserie* (page 135)
'take-away' – *la rôtisserie* (page 156); see also *la charcuterie* (page 132)
tobacconist – *le tabac* (page 156)

La banque – *the bank*

Opening hours, and even opening days, can vary from town to town. One has to check these, and the imminence of public holidays. See the French time-table on page 18. Otherwise there should be no problem about currency exchange, travellers' cheques and Eurocheques. One needs to see one's home bank about the Eurocheque encashment card.

Long-term visitors might consider opening a French account. The French still suffer from fairly rigorous exchange regulations. While these continue, non-residents cannot open bank accounts in the normal sense. But if one is going to visit France regularly, especially if one plans always to return to the same district, it might be worth opening *un compte étranger* – a non-resident's account. Basically (but there are a few loop-holes) any currency *except* French francs can be paid in, while *only* French francs can be withdrawn. Thus transfers of sterling can be made from one's British bank whenever one wants to; these are converted by the French bank into francs. A French cheque book allows unlimited withdrawals at one's 'home' branch, 3000 francs a week at other branches; and a credit card will allow withdrawal of up to 1800 francs at 24-hour cash dispensers. Cheques are easily accepted in France, upon proof of identity (passport), perhaps because it is a criminal offence to write a cheque if one's account cannot stand it (in Britain it is a civil offence). No interest is paid by the bank, but there are no bank charges except for a credit card. This sort of account is no good for dumping one's roulette winnings, but frequent visitors find it more convenient than bothering with travellers' cheques and so forth. Up-to-date details can be obtained from any French bank.

La blanchisserie; nettoyage à sec – *laundry and dry cleaning*

Blanchisseries are usually hand laundries, fairly expensive, doing a careful job with delicate garments. No need to make a list: put the stuff on the counter piece by piece and the list will be made for you. *La blanchisserie* often doubles with the *nettoyage à sec*; for the latter, fortunately, most garments are now marked with international symbols showing what sol-vents, etc., may be used. No linguistic problems; a price list is usually on the wall *(C'est combien?* – How much is it?) but make sure you know when it will be ready.

C'est urgent – 'It's urgent.'

Inutile après mercredi – 'No deal if it can't be done by Wednesday.'

Le dernier délai, c'est mercredi – 'Wednesday is the last possible day.'

Launderettes (washeterias) are few and far between. Everybody has a washing machine these days – there are cheap portable plastic ones on the market. Still, you might ask at the tourist office: *est-ce qu'il y a une blanchisserie automatique?*

If you are in a village *gîte* you will probably see *le lavoir* near the spring or down by the river: a communal clothes-washing place, with individual stone or concrete troughs and sloping surfaces for scrubbing and pounding. The ladies of my village all have *machines à laver*, but they still use *le lavoir*, on the grounds that there is nothing like a good final rinse in 50 gallons of clear spring water. Next to the *lavoir* there are the municipal washing lines; the last theft from those (a sheet) was in 1956 and they're still talking about it. The *lavoir* is free, and you are perfectly entitled to use it – in fact you will be welcome, and it's a good opportunity for breaking down social barriers. Doing the smalls before breakfast in cold water can be quite an agreeable experience on a fine summer's morning . . . and they'll be dry by eleven. (This is the Midi, of course – we southerners shudder at the thought of what might be the plight of the sneezing inhabitants of drizzly Brittany.)

La boucherie – *the butcher's shop*

The midday meal on Sunday is the gastronomic high-spot of the week. Consequently, *le boucher* opens his shop on Sunday morning (like *le pâtissier*) but will take Monday morning, or all day Monday, as a time for rest. But the supermarket and hypermarket *rayons de boucherie*, like the other counters of those establishments, will be closed on Sunday and open on Monday.

Le boucher sells beef (*le boeuf*), veal (*le veau*), and lamb (*le mouton*, i.e. 'mutton', unless it is very young, small and milk-fed, when it is *agneau*, m., lamb. Most British and New Zealand 'lambs' are youngish *moutons.*). He usually sells pork (*le porc*) though strictly speaking that is the business of the *charcuterie*. He may well sell poultry (*les volailles*, f.) though you may find a specialist *volailles* shop. He might extend his range through many of the *charcuterie*'s products. He sells game (*le gibier*) in season. He does not, however, sell horse meat. That is sold only at the specialist *boucherie chevaline* which clearly announces itself as such, often with a splendid gilded horse's head outside. (A fair amount of horse meat is sold in France. It is not particularly cheap. Some people prefer it, and claim that it is less likely to have been raised on artificial hormones than beef, and especially veal.)

French butchers have a more fiddly job than British ones. They cut up the animal along the muscles, producing 'joints' that are free from fat, gristle, integuments and (for many pieces) bones. Thus you will not find the British sirloin, which is a cross-section including a bit of *filet*, a bit of *contre-filet*, a bit of *bavette* and a T-shaped bone. You will find those three elements, dissected lengthways: fillet steak, sirloin steak (trimmed more neatly than in Britain) and *bavette* steak, which is cheaper than the others but – after the butcher has removed the connective tissue and fat – makes a very acceptable steak. The typical beef piece for roasting is *le rosbif*: a long muscle carefully de-fatted and then barded with a thin sheet of hard pork fat, tied on with loops of string; particularly suitable if you have a spit-roasting oven.

Steak, *le bifteck*, can come from many parts of the animal. Fillet steak, the most expensive, will hardly be called *bifteck*; it is *le filet*. There are some odd steaks known as *morceaux du boucher*, the butcher's bits: *araignée, onglet, merlan* . . . You are unlikely to be rewarded with these until you are a regular, but if you ask for *de l'araignée* it shows you know what's what: inexpensive and odd-looking, it is fairly tender and has a good flavour.

Minced meat (*le haché*), except pork sausage meat, is minced for each individual customer. *Boeuf haché* should be free of fat and gristle. After the butcher has minced your purchase, in a machine that cuts finely rather than squeezing and extruding, he will – if you ask for *des steaks hachés* – mould it into hamburger-sized ovals. To make your own pâté is simple: beef, lean pork, fat pork and so on will be minced for you.

Those who want to do some loving and careful cookery in the *gîte*, inspired by Elizabeth David or other admirable writers, will know the proper words and descriptions and should certainly tell the butcher what they propose to cook. Stewing steak is called *le boeuf bourguignon*, and it can be bought as such; but if you say *je veux faire du boeuf bourguignon* a (free) piece of pork skin (*couenne*, pronounced kwan) will usually be offered. This, cooked with the meat, and later removed, will add *onctuosité*, unctuousness, to the dish. A chunk of marrow-bone (*un os à moelle*, pronounced mwal) might be suggested too. And in general it can be assumed that the butcher knows about cooking; take him into your confidence about what you propose to do; mistakes will be avoided and experience gained. Never hesitate to ask *qu'est-ce que c'est? qu'est-ce qu'on en fait?* – 'What's that? What does one do with it?'

> *Du —— pour griller* – some —— to grill
> *Du —— pour faire à la poêle* (pronounced pwal) – some ——
> to cook with minimum fat in the frying-pan
> *pour un ragoût* – for a stew
> *pour bouillir/pour un pot-au-feu* – for boiling

Offal is cheaper in Britain than in France, because so many Britons have never learned the often tedious ways of cooking it. Sweetbreads, hearts, trotters and so forth have a higher market value in France. Sophie does brains beautifully; in the seventies her Cornish butcher gave them to her free (in a rather messy state). They cost a lot in France; deep-frozen sheep's brains are the only part of the New Zealand animal to get there. If you are not a connoisseur of variety meats (that's American for an offal-nosher) you will not be experimenting in *gîte* or tent; but as a keen c. of v. m. I earnestly advise adventures in a good restaurant. *Tripes à la mode de Caen* can hardly be repeated back in Britain – British tripe always turns out slithery and yucky, perhaps because of the way such non-U stuff is prepared by the butcher. Quite U in France, though. General de Gaulle was, and I am, very partial to a nice grilled trotter (*un pied de porc grillé*) but it's really restaurant food, being a lot of bother to do properly. Au Pied de Cochon, in Paris, is such a big restaurant that it can't do any harm if I mention it: there, a dozen oysters and a *plateau de Saint-Antoine* – foot, ear and tail, with chips – is an experience that the intrepid traveller might attempt. The best pig's foot I ever ate, though, was in London, at the Escargot in Greek Street, and it cost the same as fillet steak. That was years ago, under the old management – I don't know if they still do it.

Poultry: *un poulet fermier* – a farmer's, or free-range, chicken – costs a lot more than *un poulet ordinaire*. It does not fall to bits in a cloud of steam, and is in fact less tender. If it is a good one (*les poulets de Bresse* are excellent, and sometimes exported from the Bresse region near Lyon) it has a different taste. In the butcher's shop or the specialist *volailles* shop, birds will probably come with feet, head and all innards intact including guts. If sold as *effilé*, just the guts have been removed; liver, heart, etc., are in place. *PAC* (usually seen on the label of supermarket birds) means *prêt à cuire* – oven-ready. If you don't want to cope with much preparation, ask *voulez-vous le préparer, s'il vous plaît?* – will you please prepare it?

Up-market from the chicken is *la pintade*, the guinea-fowl, which is very popular in France. It has drier flesh than chicken and is good pot-roasted; if oven-roasting, baste copiously and often.

Rabbit (*le lapin*) is well thought of. The ones you see ready skinned and ready to be cooked are tame ones, raised for the table. Wild rabbits are highly prized; in the hypermarket there are deep-frozen ones, in fur and all, expensively imported from Britain.

Halves (*la moitié* . . .) of chickens, rabbits, etc., can usually be bought. And quarters (*le quart*, pronounced car) of turkey (*la dinde*). But turkey is usually battery-raised. A real *dinde fermière* is hard to find, and very dear.

Real French Foodies get their beef, mutton and pork from the butcher, but know a little farm up in the hills where they get their poultry. You might pass one advertising *volailles* . . . and they might expect you to take the thing away squawking.

La boulangerie – *the baker's shop*

What boiled potatoes are to the Briton, and rice to the Indian, bread is, or was, to the Frenchman. It mops up the gravy. Less is being eaten now than formerly, because of prosperity, but the French still want it freshly made, which means not more than eight hours old. Long ago the French baker got four hours' sleep at night and a couple of hours in the afternoon, but nowadays, since industrial workers do a 39-hour week, he objects to putting in much more than 60 hours in his family business. So shortcuts are taken, and French bread is often not what it was. Nevertheless, a *boulanger* produces hot, freshly baked loaves once or twice a day, and they are fine when they are still warm and crusty. Britons have revolted against wrapped sliced muck fit only for the pop-up toaster, and can often get a wide variety of brown and white 'real' bread from the local bakery; the average French product may be less good, but do shop around and experiment. There are lots and lots of *boulangeries*, and, being French and individual, they are all different; as well as the normal white loaf, sold at a lowish controlled price, bakers now make – at higher prices – various special loaves, which can be excellent.

Bakers close one day a week, but in a small town they never all close on the same day.

The usual name for a small white loaf a couple of feet long and about three inches in diameter is *la baguette* (the wand). Other names for a variety of sizes and shapes vary from place to place (*le bâtard, la flûte, la ficelle* . . .). No problem: they are all on show, and one points to the loaf one wants and says *un pain comme cela, s'il vous plaît* – a loaf like that, please.

Non-standard loaves can be sold at a higher price per unit of weight. These may be in fancy shapes (one of our local bakers is a dab hand at turning out alligators when he feels like it) or have special ingredients or different baking methods. Generalisation is impossible. However:

pain au levain is raised in an old-fashioned way, is often chewier and remains eatable longer;
pain de campagne looks very hand-made; can be good;
pain complet is made with wholemeal flour;
pain de seigle includes rye flour;
pain au son has added bran, for fibre-addicts;
pain cuit au feu de bois is baked in a wood-fired oven, which can make a perceptible difference.

A normal French loaf, sliced across, produces slices with big holes through which jam drips on fingers and clothes. Cut off a six-inch length and slice it into two, lengthways – and, if you like, remove some of the crumb. The crust of these half-cylinders is jam-proof. That is the way to make sandwiches, too.

Croissants – not what they were, unless *au beurre*, made with butter – are bought at *la boulangerie*; and sometimes the simpler sort of cakes. For more elegant cakes and pastries, go to the *pâtisserie*.

Un dépôt de pain is a place where bread is sold but not made on the premises. Shunned by the French, unless they live in a village too small to have its own *boulanger*. Supermarkets are usually *dépôts de pain*, selling loaves made by a local *boulanger*. They may also have small supplies of factory-made, wrapped sliced bread, often sweetish in flavour, and hardly ever bought except for making *croque-monsieur*: toasted sandwiches. If you do buy such an un-French loaf, inspect it carefully for signs of mould under the cellophane and look for the 'sell by' date – *la date limite de vente*.

German-made pumpernickel can be found on the shelves of big supermarkets; and Ryvita-like crispbreads. Packets of *pains azymes* contain matzo-type biscuits, the thinner sort being like Carr's water biscuits.

La charcuterie – *the pork butcher's, the delicatessen*

Jane Grigson's *Charcuterie and French Pork Cookery* contains an excellent short introduction to this inexhaustible subject. I would differ from her on a few points, but that is because she and I have patronised perhaps only fifty or a hundred *charcuteries* out of the thousands in France. Each *charcutier* has his own specialities; so does each region. Mrs Grigson, I think, knows the *charcuteries* of the Loire valley best; down where I live there is more emphasis on ham, and flights of inventive genius are fewer; many people say (and many vigorously deny) that true appreciation of *charcuterie* can be acquired only by a lifetime of study within a small radius of Lyon.

The word comes from *chair cuite*, or cooked meat, but uncooked items are sold there too, and they do not all come from the pig. Pies, take-away dishes to be heated up (one place I know does a delicious home-made *coq-au-vin*, and another does a good paella with chicken and prawns) and other temptations can be found, depending on the skill, fancy and acumen of those in charge.

Basically, one should find:

le porc – pork, raw, salted and unsalted (*cru*, *salé* and *frais*). Joints of fresh pork are skinned: alas, no crackling. One up to the British.

le jambon – ham. *Jambon de Paris* or *jambon glacé* resembles British ham. A ham is a rear leg; the wicked British sell 'shoulder ham'; the French call this *épaule glacée*.

jambon cru is smoked ham eaten raw; expensive; can be delicious (very good at the start of a meal, with canteloupe melon). Ham can be bought by the single slice (*une tranche*).

poitrine salée, *poitrine fumée* – bacon, unsmoked and smoked; streaky only. In the supermarket, packed in plastic, what is called *bacon* may be on sale: this is the thinly sliced lean smoked 'eye', and is very dear. *Poitrine* will be sliced for you. It usually goes into stews in little chunks, so if you want to fry rashers, insist on its being cut thin – *très très mince*.

sausages . . . This is a vast subject. The mention of sausages (rather than, say, lamb chops; or, in arithmetic lessons, oranges) causes giggling among British schoolchildren, but the French take sausages seriously. One up to them.

la saucisse fraîche, or *la saucisse de Toulouse*, is like the British sausage in the way that Tolstoy is like Enid Blyton. It is made of 100 per cent pure pork, coarsely minced, so that the bits of lean and fat can be seen. It tastes of meat. If the standard British banger were to be sold in France it could not legally be called *saucisse*, because as well as a modest amount of meat it contains stuff called butcher's rusk (bread) and something gooey to hold as much water as possible. *Saucisse* is long; one can buy a four-foot length and coil it neatly for grilling. Sophie likes to de-fat ours by poaching it gently in fifty-fifty wine and water, after pricking it thoroughly; then grilling it fiercely, or serving it cold. The contents are sold as *chair à saucisse*, sausage meat.

There are other *saucisses* that look rather like British ones, but some of these are not for frying or grilling but for boiling in hearty soups, etc.: *saucisses de Montbéliard, missons* . . .

saucisson sec is salami-type sausage, to be eaten as it is, in slices. There are many kinds, some with wonderful names (*Jésus* and *rosette* around Lyon). If a *charcutier* has a number of different kinds he will be only too glad (if he is worth his salt) to sell you a selection – a slice or two of each, so that you can evaluate his work seriously.

boudins noirs are black puddings. Colossal variations, sometimes immense delight. Some have onions, some are made with chestnut flour, some have cream, some great gobbets of fat, some no fat at all, some have pine-nuts and raisins, some can be eaten 'raw' (they are all pre-cooked), most are best grilled gently and eaten when the skin is crisp, with mashed potatoes, sliced apples cooked in a little butter, and French mustard. Do not despise the *boudin*! Collect specimens from four or five *charcutiers* and have a *boudin*-tasting feast.

boudins blancs are the aristocratic relations of British white puddings. Even greater price range than with *boudins noirs*, because the ingredients (pork; veal? chicken breast? truffles?) can vary enormously. Grill gently. In some regions these luxury items appear only at Christmas – when, with oysters and champagne, they form the traditional snack after midnight mass.

andouillettes are sausages made of pig's tripe. Arthur Eperon's dog doesn't like them, nor does Mr Eperon. General de Gaulle loved them, and so do I; but not from every *charcutier*. I earnestly beseech you to buy a pair, from two different shops, prick and grill very gently, serve very hot on a hot plate with good mustard . . . if unconvinced, bad luck; otherwise, you will have found an intense new physical pleasure and I shall not have lived in vain.

andouilles, to *andouillettes*, are what *saucisson sec* is to *saucisse fraîche*: hard, to be sliced and eaten cold.

pâtés of many kinds, *galantines*, *rillettes*, which could be grossly translated as kinds of meat loaf and meat pastes; different sorts of brawn (infinitely nicer than the stuff sold under that name in Britain, and of course dearer) called *hure* and *fromage de tête*; *fricandeaux*, *gayettes* and other creations may be on display, with various pies (*pâtés en croûte*) . . .

Blessed is he who finds a good *charcuterie* with a kindly *charcutière* behind the counter. Thrice blessed is he who buys in a spirit of cheerful critical adventure.

Coiffure – *hairdressing* (le coiffeur, la coiffeuse: *hairdresser, m. and f.*)

Gentlemen who need a haircut will ask for *une coupe* and resist attempts to give them *un shampooing* and other titivations. 'My hair' is *mes cheveux*, plural; *mon cheveu* would mean 'my one solitary hair', a do-it-yourself job.

As for ladies: in Britain many department stores have hairdressing salons, and in small towns there will usually be two or three hairdressers employing, say, three or four girls. The French situation is different. In our nearest small town (6000 inhabitants) there are eight salons, each consisting of one *Madame* and one *petite*. For a wash and set an appointment – *un rendezvous* – is unnecessary except at rush periods (just before 14 July, 15 August, Christmas and New Year). In larger towns Madame might have three or four *petites*; again, hardly any need for *un rendezvous*, but at rush periods they might not do their best for non-regulars. Sophie is full of praise for French hairdressers.

a trim – *une coupe*
a wash and blow dry – *un shampooing et un brushing*
a wash and set – *une mise en plis*
a bit shorter – *un peu plus court*
a parting – *une raie*

Prices should be clearly visible in the window. There is a wide price range. A tip is given to *la petite*.

Sophie has not seen a manicurist at the hairdresser's. They are found at *salons de beauté* (three in our one-horse town) where *visagistes* massage faces, apply mud packs or strawberry purée and pull out eyebrows in exchange for wads of banknotes.

La confiserie – *the sweet shop*

Do you like real hand-made chocolates? Confectionery made with real liqueurs, egg-yolks and almonds? Do you pop in to Charbonnel and Walker's whenever you stroll down Bond Street? Rejoice! Every town in France has a luxury confection-er's, and £5 or £10 will be enough for a sinfully exquisite little package. The French get one twice a year, if they are lucky, but you have only a limited time in France. . . .

By 'the French' I mean French adults. These things are far too good for the immature. French children get factory-made confectionery, from the *épicerie* or the supermarket. But not every day. Sweets do not form a regular part of the French child's diet. If your children are convinced that a daily visit to the tuck-shop is part of their birthright, give them some sweet money, show them the *confiserie* and the supermarket, and let them choose between one ounce of elegance and a bag of Mars bars made in France.

La crémerie – *the dairy*

La crèmerie sells butter, cheese, cream and whatever else the individual shopkeeper wants to stock. We haven't got a *crèmerie* down our way, because there aren't any local cows, but up in Normandy and elsewhere the gourmets (nine-tenths of the population) don't buy their dairy products at the supermarket.

Butter is taken seriously. In 1985 *Que Choisir?* (it corresponds to *Which?*) used a panel of tasters (*dégustateurs*) to judge twenty-four samples, including factory-wrapped packets and butter bought from the mound in *crèmeries*. They were looking for pronounced butter flavour and the absence of the tendency to stick to the palate. Butter-fanciers should emulate them, especially when they see it in mounds. There is a choice between salted and unsalted (*le beurre salé, doux*), pasteurised or 'raw' (*pasteurisé, cru*) and indeed *appellation contrôlée* (as with wine) and others.

In France, margarine is not coloured yellow. Eight brands of margarine were included, and the test was done under red light so as to conceal the difference. All the tasters could tell French butter from margarine, which is rarely used as a substitute. However, 'low-fat' margarines have recently caught slimmers' fancy, as a breakfast spread.

Foodies know about the difference between *crème fraîche* and British-type cream. *Crème fraîche* has a nutty taste and is more useful in cooking. British-type cream can be found in the *épicerie* as *crème stérilisée*.

Milk: see *l'épicerie* (page 138).

As for cheese, don't think I'm lazy. I spent most of today and all yesterday on a preparatory outline for a section on French cheeses; realised that much of it would be cribbed from existing publications (I know fifty French cheeses, but only fifteen intimately); and tore it up. There is no such thing as *cheese*, there are only cheeses. Many different kinds are made in France, both in factories and on farms. No meal is complete without a go at some cheeses, with a glass of red wine, before the sweet course; some cheeses are best in the summer, some in the winter; some come from the mountain, others from the lush meadow; some are made from cow's milk, some from ewe's or goat's milk (*fromage de vache, de brebis, de chèvre*). Demure, aggressive, big, little, queer, orthodox, in simple youth and in full-blown ripeness – custom cannot stale the infinite variety of a good French cheese board. Always try unfamiliar ones, and do ask their names at the restaurant.

The French consider it unnecessary, or sacrilegious, to import much cheese. Parmesan is hard to find. But they do have matured Dutch Edam (in Britain one usually finds only the young bland sort). This is called *étuvé* (less mature Edam is *demi-étuvé*) and grates well, as a fair substitute for parmesan. For *gratins* they use soft French-made Emmenthaler and call it *Gruyère* (which it isn't).

If you pass near Millau, make a short detour to Roquefort and take a free trip down the cool damp cheese mine (the attendants will lend you a warm cloak if you're dressed for hot weather).

A word of warning: clumps of wanderers from outside France have taken to settling in the wilder parts, complete with a nanny-goat or two. They attempt to flog ecological-looking flat round goat's-milk cheeses (*fromage pur chèvre*) to the hated bourgeoisie who pass in motor cars. The selling point is *naturalness*, and naturally you may get a touch of brucellosis. Beware.

No cheese in the *crémerie?* Then there is *une fromagerie* almost next door.

La droguerie

La droguerie does not sell drugs. (Medicines are the business of *la pharmacie.*) It sells paint (*la peinture*), all sorts of household cleaning materials (*produits d'entretien*), the French equivalent of methylated spirits (*alcool à brûler*), bleach (*eau de Javel*), soap (*le savon*, household, and *la savonette*, toilet), the cheaper kinds of make-up, aerosols of insecticide (*bombes* . . . Néocide is one make), *jerricans* (m.) for wine, corks (*bouchons*, m.) and a whole range of products such as might be on sale in a British ironmonger's – except tools, etc., made of metal (which are the business of *la quincaillerie*). A general oddment shop. Ours sells string and sealing-wax (big lumps, for melting in an old saucepan and dipping the necks of filled wine-bottles in, if one plans to keep the wine for a decade).

L'épicerie – *the grocery*

A small *épicerie* might be called *une alimentation générale*. Almost all such places have turned themselves into self-service stores (see page 118); this section deals with things found on the supermarket's *épicerie* shelves.

Wine: see page 173
Beer: see page 191
Butter and cheese: see page 136
Fresh fruit and vegetables: see page 143

See also other relevant sections for other fresh food and ready-prepared dishes; the bigger supermarkets and of course the hypermarkets have departments for these things.

Most of what is on sale is obvious. Here are some notes on less obvious things.

Few French people drink milk (*le lait*) after weaning, except at breakfast as an ingredient in *café au lait* or *chocolat*. For cookery (mainly desserts) they usually buy UHT long-life milk; it comes in cardboard litre *briques* or plastic bottles. There are enough animal fats in their diet, so they buy *lait écrémé* (skimmed) or *demi-écrémé* (semi-skimmed) – green or blue tops on the bottles. *Lait entier* (red top) is full-cream. If they want cream in their recipes they buy it as such (*crème fraîche*). But *lait frais* – fresh milk – can sometimes be found (less often in the Midi), both *pasteurisé* and raw (*cru*).

Those who like cow's milk as a tipple are better off elsewhere, but the *épicerie* is a good place for yoghourt (*le yaourt*).

Dried milk (*lait en poudre*, e.g. Quicklait, Régilait) is easily found, both *écrémé* and *entier*, and is handy for campers; so is condensed milk (*lait concentré*) in tins and in convenient tubes like toothpaste.

Limonades are soft drinks (lemonade is *citronnade*). There are many of these, some in litre bottles (returnable – see beer, page 191). Even Coca-Cola. Pschitt and Sic are good inexpensive lemonades, but one does get tired of children's witticisms about those brand names after the first fortnight. For dilution there are excellent fruit syrups (*sirops*) in great variety.

Cognac, whisky, etc., are obvious.

Tea: see page 110. If you have to buy some *thé* (pronounced tay), try to get *pur ceylan*.

Coffee (*le café*): comes in vacuum packets, usually 250g (½ lb). *Moulu* is ground, *en grains* is unground. If the variety of bean is *Arabica* it is proudly proclaimed. *Robusta* gives a cheaper, full-bodied breakfast brew. *Café décaféiné* (decafeinated) can be found, both real and instant.

Oil: cooking oil should be your frying medium (infinitely more convenient, anyway, under canvas); butter is a mess when it's hot, lard is not easily found and is used only for special purposes, and margarine is margarine. As for the *huiles*, sunflower (*tournesol*) and ground-nut (*arachide* – but peanuts themselves are called *cacahuètes*, pronounced ca-ca-wet) are good, but there are others. Small print on the bottles usually shows the maximum temperature the oil can be raised to before changing its character (or bursting into flame); *huile pour friture* is for frying; *huile pour assaisonnement* is the poor man's substitute for olive oil with salads, and is *not* for frying.

Of course the queen of oils is olive oil, and olive oil bores have been well dealt with in *The Official Foodie Handbook*. I am a relentless olive oil bore; I take a spoonful of the finest local *huile d'olive, première pression à froid,* put it in an eggcup and freeze it. Then I eat it on bits of brown bread. Mmm! Polyunsaturated too! Enough, except to say that the finest olive oil is really quite cheap in France (a litre bottle holds the equivalent of over 2 lb of butter) so don't cheat yourself by making do with Spanish *huile raffinée. Raffinée* means mucked about with in factories. *Fruitée* means strong-tasting, *douce* is more neutral in taste. Olive oil is *pour friture, pour assaisonnement* and *pour* rubbing all over yourself. If you are where olives, vines and wheat flourish you are at the heart of civilisation; make something better than hay while the sun shines.

Vinegar: the best *vinaigre de vin,* wine vinegar, is ridiculously cheap. Only masochists should use anything else in France (in England too, for that matter, but it's dearer there than harsh acids made from something else). It can be bought flavoured with various things (*framboise,* raspberry, was all the rage some years ago, for making sweet-sour sauces). What green salad needs is three or four parts of good olive oil to one part of best plain wine vinegar, a little salt, and nothing else.

Flour (*la farine*) is normally sold plain, not self-raising. Baking powder is sold in small sachets as *levure alsacienne.* Dried baker's yeast comes in similar sachets: *levure de boulangerie.* (Some bakers sell it fresh if one asks nicely.)

Some cooks use potato flour (*fécule de pomme de terre*) for soufflés, and for thickening transparent sauces; it comes in 250g (½ lb) packets.

Cornflour is *Maizena,* in similar packets.

Breadcrumbs, for egg-and breadcrumbing things, are in smaller packets: *la chapelure.*

Sugar (*le sucre*) comes *en morceaux* (lump), *en poudre* (granulated) and *à glacer* (icing). *La cassonade* is brown sugar. Lumps of brownish sugar, *sucre roux,* made by Cossé-Duval, come in a beautifully Victorian box. Eat the contents and take the box home as a souvenir.

Eggs are obvious (*les oeufs*), but let us get the pronunciation right. In the singular the *f* is heard; roughly 'erf'. *Un oeuf* is as good as a feast, ha ha. In the plural it is silent: 'er'; *six oeufs* are pronounced roughly 'see zer'. Strange but true.

Factory-made ice cream is rather better than in Britain; 'non-milk fats' are not allowed. Imaginative mixtures and presentations, in sizes for three or four portions, can be found in the deep-freeze section of big *épiceries* and supermarkets. The real stuff, made of egg-yolks, cream and fresh fruit, is found at that expensive shop *la confiserie*.

Things in tins: these are mostly obvious. Pulses – beans (*haricots*), lentils (*lentilles*) and the excellent chick-peas (*pois chiches*, not well known in Britain – one meets them in Italy as *ceci* and in Spain as *garbanzos*) – are valuable, and available in France in greater variety than in Britain. They can of course be bought dried in packets (*haricots secs*, dried beans), but as they need soaking and cooking (chick-peas need ages) they are a bother for holiday cookery. They can be bought cooked in tins, tarted up in various ways, but if you buy a tin marked *au naturel* they can be incorporated in your own recipes. As the tin says, these things *au naturel* should be rinsed in luke-warm water before use (under the tap, in a colander).

Choucroute (sauerkraut) is good in tins. If you buy a tin of *choucroute garnie* it will include bits of factory-made *charcuterie*; better to buy a tin of plain *choucroute* and ask at the *charcuterie* for a few things to go with it (ham, bacon, sausage . . .).

Tripe dishes (*tripes à la mode de Caen*, etc.) take kindly to canning. The expensive Arthus tins of *pieds et paquets marseillais* (from the sheep) are excellent. Sophie and I had never touched tripe in our lives until a French friend sent us a tin of those for Christmas when we lived in England; we regarded it with prudish suspicion but at last plucked up courage to heat and open it; we stared at each other with a wild surmise, and then found that a new planet had swum into our ken. We haven't looked back.

Plenty of tunny fish (*le thon*) in tins, both in oil (*à l'huile*) and *au naturel*; and many grades. *Thon au naturel* is useful for many dishes.

Rice (*le riz*) is grown in France, in the Camargue. We find that the Camargue type called Surinam (it doesn't come from Surinam; it's a type) is as good as the best Basmati. Very long grain.

Jam (*la confiture*) can be very good. As most of it is made of fruit, sugar and nothing else (*pur fruit, pur sucre*) it can be runnier than British factory jam, with a tendency to ferment or go mouldy two or three weeks after opening, so it is best to buy the smaller jars and keep them in the fridge.

Hardly any factory-made pies in cardboard boxes. (There are freshly made meat pies at the *charcuterie* and fruit tarts at the *pâtisserie*.)

There are many more deep-frozen articles than was the case a few years ago, but – as one might expect – not as many as in Britain. But again, as one might expect, some of the frozen convenience dishes are of high quality, and proportionately dear. As for frozen raw materials, scallops (*coquilles Saint-Jacques*) come from bonny Scotland, frogs' legs (*cuisses de grenouilles*) from Thailand and sheep's brains (*cervelles d'agneau*) from down under. As in Britain, frozen puff pastry (*pâte feuilletée*) saves a lot of trouble, but anyone should be able to rub up a bit of shortcrust (*pâte brisée*). No linguistic problems at the deep-freeze: lovely pictures. But one needs to read the packet to know if one should thaw the stuff out first (*décongeler à l'air ambiante*) or cook it while it is still *congelé*.

Supermarket *épiceries* are busiest late on Fridays; on Monday mornings the big ones (real supermarkets and hypermarkets) attract Britons, Swedes, Germans, etc., unsuitably attired in swimsuits and baffled by the fact that normal food shops are shut.

Fruits et légumes – *fruit and vegetables; and the market*

Vive la France! French-grown, and preferably local-grown, fruit and vegetables are better and cheaper than those in British shops. Thank not only the climate, the soil and the skill of the growers, but also the wisdom of French consumers. A striking difference in eating habits in France and Britain is that the French insist on having fresh vegetables and green salads daily. Not that they are vegetarians; far from it. But the British starch-fat-sugar emphasis is absent. (Figures from the late seventies for consumption per head of the population, per year are: vegetables other than potatoes: UK 74kg, France 119kg; potatoes, UK 100kg, France 84kg; meat, UK 76kg, France 108kg.)

Three cheers for England! We have the best cookery books in the world (and perhaps the greatest number; more cookbooks than hot dinners?). Jane Grigson's *Vegetable Book* plus a French market spells happiness. Over 600 pages, artichokes to yams, via *poivrons, potirons* and *mâche* (sweet peppers, pumpkins and lamb's lettuce) – yes, the French names are in the index as well as the English ones, because Mrs Grigson sensibly spends a lot of time in France.

Vegetarians are not well catered for in French restaurants; an omelette, a vegetable course and a dessert, *à la carte*, are not such good value as a *table d'hôte* menu. Only a tiny minority of French people exclude meat from their diet. But on a self-catering holiday vegetarians will be in clover, if that's the *mot juste*.

Of course there are shops for *fruits et légumes*. Many *épiceries* sell a selection, and there will be a lot in the supermarket. But the best place is the market proper. There, one can emulate the conscientious *ménagère* (housewife) as she goes the rounds of the stalls, comparing quality and price. Items are clearly marked with the price, usually by the kilo.

Those who are keen on comparing British and French prices will have worked out the conversion factor at the start of their holiday: divide 1 by the number of francs to the £, and divide the result by 2.2; this converts a price of 1 franc per kilo into £s per pound; at 11 francs to the £, £0.04. Easier to multiply the francs by 100 (thus getting into centimes, or old francs) which gives the result in pence per pound: 1 franc per kilo = 4p per lb (at F11 = £1). Of course nothing is as cheap as one franc a kilo; this sum, worked out once, gives you the conversion factor: 4, in this case. So at 7 francs per kilo you know you are paying 28 pence per pound. Pop the conversion factor into your pocket calculator's memory, and there you are, if that sort of thing sends you. Personally, I'd leave my calculator at home, and opt for a pocket full of change, a big shopping bag, Jane Grigson's book and a lot of vitamin-rich fun.

Remember that you do *not* have to buy a whole kilo of anything. In Britain one is used to asking the greengrocer for a pound of this and a half-pound of that. Watch the French shopper: she or he picks out just the number of tomatoes, sweet peppers and peaches she wants, looking at them carefully; she puts them into the plastic bowl provided, and the stall-holder weighs them. But in a market he probably won't wrap them; you need a good shopping bag (*un sac à provisions*, or a net bag, *un filet*, from *la droguerie* and elsewhere). Perhaps there are items the merchant does not want handled and poked. In that case he will keep them out of range – they might be very early expensive peaches or melons. Ask for them by ones and twos. Just watch what goes on. In the case of French beans (*haricots verts*), real peas in pods (*petits pois*) and those delicious flat peas you eat pod and all after stringing if necessary (*pois mange-tout* or *gourmands*), buy them by the (good) pound, *la livre*, or in smaller quantities: 200g (*deux cent grammes*), 300g, or just put as many as you want into the bowl.

This is not a cookery book. But a few small points. I suppose everybody knows that foreign growers, in Spain, Israel and elsewhere, grow specially tasteless tomatoes for the British market, since British wholesalers insist on appearance rather than flavour. There are delicious varieties that are bumpy and ridgy, and they have been ripened on the plant. The same goes for short stumpy cucumbers. But choose what is in season and what is local. France is still a country of local traditions, and things that are highly appreciated and well grown in one smallish area may not be so good elsewhere. Marketing experts (I mean people in city offices, not housewives planning a good meal) say that France has not yet got an efficient distribution system. By this they mean that the produce does not go all the way to Paris and back again; a lot of it goes straight to the local market and the local shops.

A good market is a fascinating place, and not just for fruit and vegetables. A sad gap in the Michelin guides is that neither the red one nor the green ones tell us when is market day. *C'est quand, le marché?* is a basic question as soon as one arrives somewhere. In biggish towns there is a covered market-hall, open every day, or every morning (don't forget that the morning ends around midday, and that the keen shopper was there before 9 a.m.). Luckily Michelin has a symbol for the market-hall on the town plans.

Paris has markets too. Everyone has heard of the *rue Mouffetard*, which has turned into a tourist attraction and is on the postcards. The canny Parisienne goes to the twice-weekly market in the Place Monge, five minutes away.

Ordinary French people are honest. There is less need to worry about short-changing, pickpockets and bag-snatchers in a small French town than in London. However, if you are in a resort or a market where tourists cluster (lots of cheapjacks, few housewives), especially if the tourists go about unsuitably dressed (one does not normally expose the navel in mid-town, unless one is a fat-bellied male festooned with cameras and has been photographing very old ladies because they look 'picturesque' or 'quaint') and seem to have more money than is good for them – that is where it is well to exercise prudence. In such places I try to compensate for my finely chiselled Home Counties features by digging out my beret, carrying a long loaf under my arm and sticking an extinguished Gauloise to my lower lip; but as fewer and fewer Frenchmen look like that nowadays I am probably taken for a member of the dreaded British Intelligence Service on a secret mission.

La librairie – *the bookshop*

The library is *la bibliothèque*, the bookshop is *la librairie*. France is poorly off for public libraries, compared with Britain. But there are plenty of bookshops. Only specialist bookshops in Paris and other large centres have any stock of English-language books, and they carry a big mark-up. French books in France are somewhat cheaper than English books in Britain, largely because hard covers are not usual.

Out-of-date articles on France may suggest that it is cheaper to buy best-sellers like the Michelin guide from hypermarkets. For a short period that was the case, but now, as in Britain, retail price maintenance is in force, to protect the smaller bookseller who performs a public service by stocking less popular books as well as those that sell quickly.

La mercerie – *the haberdashery*

This shop, usually a small one run by a lady with plenty of time for gossip and advice, sells stuff for first-aid to clothing: buttons (*le bouton*), zip fasteners (*la fermeture éclair*), pins (*l'epingle*, f.), safety pins (*l'é. de nourrice*, i.e. wet-nurses' pins), needles (*l'aiguille*, f.), thread (*le fil*) and other oddments for which you will need either a dictionary or the word *le machin* (see page 43) and gestures.

Some items from the range are sold in the supermarket in transparent plastic packs – language unnecessary.

The lady in *la mercerie* is of course a source of information about home dressmakers who will perform alterations or run you up a chic or un-chic little creation.

La pâtisserie – *the cake shop*

A better translation is 'the pastrycook's'. Cake exists, called *le cake*, pronounced kak, but is more usually found factory-made on supermarket shelves – imitation Dundee cake, etc. *Le pâtissier* or *la pâtissière* go in for pastry: fruit tarts *(la tarte aux fruits)*, éclairs and so on. No language problem: it's all visible and freshly made. If one worries about the waistline it is essential to avert the gaze from that sinfully tempting window.

Birthday cakes are made to order, but do write the inscription out in capital letters. Even then, JOHN will perhaps appear as JHON, but it's just as nice to eat.

The big time is Sunday morning: people buy fresh fruit tarts for the week's best meal.

La pharmacie – *the chemist's shop*

La pharmacie is there, primarily, to supply medical items. Cameras, films, postcards, liquidisers, transistor radios, cassettes and so forth are sold elsewhere.

There is a large green cross outside the shop, usually illuminated when it is open. If the *pharmacie* is closed, a notice on the door says where the 'duty' *pharmacie* is to be found – *la pharmacie de garde*.

Chain chemists are illegal. Each *pharmacien* or *pharmacienne* is responsible for his or her own shop, and answerable for any blunders committed. *Pharmacien(ne)s* are well qualified, and many people go to them in the first instance if they are feeling *fatigué* (which in spoken French means ill, not tired) or if they have suffered some minor injury. But the *pharmacien* would not dream of suggesting a treatment if there were the slightest chance that a doctor might be needed. The properly insured visitor will prefer to consult a doctor (who is incidentally more likely to speak English) but – since there are so many *pharmacies* clearly visible in main streets – it is practical, if one does not know a town, to go to the *pharmacie* in the first instance. One will be told where the nearest doctor is, and the happy *pharmacien* knows that one will soon be back with a prescription. (See page 166 for chapter on visiting the doctor.)

France is as severe as Britain in classifying drugs as 'prescription only'. For minor matters, when the emergency kit has run out, go to *la pharmacie* for the things on this page and for aspirin, *l'aspirine* (f.). If you cannot take aspirin (*Je ne supporte pas l'aspirine; supporter* means to tolerate) you want a painkiller, *une analgésique*. But the most effective are on prescription. Many of these, by the way, are in suppository form. Despite appearances, it is logical to insert a headache remedy up one's rear if the active ingredient is absorbed in the bowel, and the French, who take their stomachs very seriously, are keen prescribers and inserters of *suppositoires*. If you refuse this simple method of medication (*je ne supporte pas les suppositoires*) something else will be suggested, but for heaven's sake don't try swallowing *une suppositoire*; that would be putting the cart before the horse.

The preferred antiseptic is alcohol, at 90° – *l'alcool* (m.) *à quatre-vingt-dix degrés*. This is of course highly inflammable: it is twice the strength of normal brandy and whisky. It is perfectly drinkable if you water it down; equal parts of water and alcohol at 90° produce vodka (a tasteless neutral spirit) at 45°. That is why it is on sale only at the chemist's, who is supposed not to sell it in larger quantities than a quarter of a litre. When the locals make their own liqueurs, with cherries, verbena leaves or other things, they are supposed to go to the *épicerie* and buy *alcool blanc pour fruits* at 40°, paying the duty – it works out at about five times the price of chemists' alcohol stretched out to the same strength. Of course they don't, and the chemist is quite happy to sell a litre at a time (when he has it; he is rationed to what the authorities think are the population's reasonable antiseptic needs) to people whom he thinks safe, respectable and discreet. Like me. If you are bringing alcohol back to England as part of your booze ration, alcohol is just alcohol, whether it's 30° or 90°. It's made from wine – the great surplus wine lake – but refined to be flavourless. If you are fond of having things *flambé*, like fried bananas or Christmas pudding, a small shot of 90° in with the brandy ensures instant ignition. Be careful, though: *alcool à brûler*, sold by the *droguerie* as the equivalent of meths, is poison; so is *alcool dénaturé*. Play safe: having bought your first quarter-litre, ask the chemist *Est-ce qu'on pourrait faire des liqueurs avec?* –

'Could one make liqueurs with it?'

One day, I suppose, the authorities will crack down, and *alcool à 90°* will cease to be the preferred antiseptic. So please play safe.

The chemist also sells:

elastoplast – *pansements adhésifs, sparadrap*
baby food in little pots – *petits pots*
throwaway nappies – *couches* (Pampers is a well-known brand)
contraceptive sheaths – *préservatifs*
contact lens lotion – *la solution pour lentilles de contact* (for wetting: *pour pose;* for cleaning: *pour nettoyage*) – also obtainable from opticians.
See also 'For women', page 157.

Useful *pharmacie* vocabulary might include:

I want a remedy for —— – *Je voudrais quelque chose pour* ——
a cold – *un rhume*
constipation – *la constipation*
a cough – *une toux*
diarrhoea – *la diarrhée*
eczema – *l'eczéma* (m.)
hay fever – *le rhume des foins*
an insect bite – *un piqûre d'insecte* (show the bite)
a sore throat – *une angine* (angina pectoris is quite a different matter, *angine de poitrine*)

La poissonnerie – *the fishmonger's*

There are fish shops in towns, fish-stalls run by travelling merchants in weekly markets, and – often best of all – permanent fish stalls in permanent markets. Naturally these are cheapest, and often best, by a fishing port. Brixham fish tends to go up to London and back again before going on sale in Brixham, but a lot of Boulogne and Sète fish goes straight from quay to customer.

A splendid sight! Down our way you need a copy of Alan Davidson's remarkable Penguin, *Mediterranean Seafood*, in order to identify many of the exhibits. Davidson gives pictures, natural history, names in all languages around the Mediterranean, simple cookery rules for each fish, and more elaborate authentic recipes; there is no book like Davidson's in any language – a labour of love, a delight to use, and a bargain.

Prices are clearly marked, per kilo. Many items are familiar. Soles and turbot (same names as in English) are international; no cheaper than in Britain. Lobster (*le homard*) and crawfish (*la langouste*) have become expense-account food, and will not often be seen on sale in the market; they go to posh restaurants and pass a few days in captivity twiddling their feelers in the aquarium in the window awaiting a well-heeled customer.

Some of the more spectacular small exhibits, delightfully ugly and highly coloured, are for making fish soups and *bouillabaisse*, not for serving as individual items. Such dishes are troublesome to prepare, and best tried first at a good restaurant.

Fresh tunny or tuna (*le thon*) catches the eye because of its size. This mighty fish is sold in steaks, which can be simply grilled. The best canned sort is perhaps better for serving cold, but once in a while an authentic slice is an agreeable experience. Alas, it is getting dearer round our way: Japanese fishmongers send great deep-freeze boats to transport Mediterranean tunny to Tokyo, where it is eaten raw and sells for ten times our local price. (It's not bad raw, actually: cut it in very thin slices and marinate in lemon juice for a few hours.)

Fresh sardines, *sardines fraîches*, and I mean fresh – bright-eyed and smelling nice – are cheap, and delicious just grilled, preferably in the open. So are fresh anchovies (*anchois*).

The octopus family, despite their exotic appeal, are nothing to write home about, as food. They all require longish preparation. But don't let me put anybody off trying them in a good fish restaurant. The octopus proper, *la poulpe*, is not on the restaurant menu: it is cheap because it is very tough. The cuttlefish, *la seiche*, turns up on menus, stewed and served in various hot-flavoured sauces. The squid, *l'encornet* (m.) whose body is a sleeve, lends itself to being stuffed with many things including sausage meat, and is quite dear in the market. Davidson is of course good on these, for those who want to have a try in their *gîte*.

Live trout (*la truite*) are on sale in most places. They are not 'wild', of course, and connoisseurs can detect a difference between the farm-bred trout fed on fish-meal and the trout you catch yourself, who has spent his time hunting flies and little fishes. But these live trout, brought to market in tanks on the merchant's lorry, are good value. You point to the ones you want, and the man nets them, clonks them on the head and weighs them. Fresh indeed!

In Sam Weller's time, oysters and poverty went together, and Dr Johnson fed them to his cat Hodge. Then they became dear in Britain and nowadays, shocking to relate, there are many Britons who have never settled down to a dozen oysters with brown bread and butter and a pint of Guinness, as a revitalising mid-morning snack. You can keep your lobsters and your smoked salmon for displays of conspicuous consumption; Sophie and I get our oysters at the oyster-beds at about £1 a dozen whenever we feel like it, which is often, and with 50p's worth of white wine, a lemon and some *pain de seigle* we're as happy as millionaires. I saved an Englishman's life with oysters once. He was contemplating suicide, in Paris. He wasn't a neurotic; in fact he had serious reason to despair. I persuaded him to come out to dinner first. He had never eaten an oyster before; we polished off a dozen each, with a bottle of Sylvaner, and then another dozen. He decided to give his troubles one more trial, after discovering this new interest in life, and with courage and a bit of luck he came through. If you have not yet taken the oyster plunge, now is the time. Oysters in France, including those from the oyster-beds by the

Mediterranean, such as the Étang (lagoon) de Thau between Sète and Agde, are officially inspected, with analyses of the water and everything, and are perfectly safe. The only danger is that you might want to go on eating oysters in England. You have to be rich to do that.

The oyster, *l'huître* (f.), comes in two basic sorts: the round flattish one (the Whitstable type), called *l'huître plate, le Belon* and other names (its official Latin name is *Ostrea edulis*); and the elongated, deeper, rougher-looking sort, *l'huître creuse*, or *la portugaise*, officially *Crassostrea angulata*. (There are many other descriptive adjectives for oysters – *claires, collées, Marennes*, the last being greenish because of the type of seaweed in their beds – but such differences are unimportant to the beginner.) *L'huître plate* is more fashionable, and more trouble to cultivate; it thus costs two or three times as much as *l'huître creuse* and is not worth the extra money.

Oysters are cheap near the oyster-beds. Elsewhere their price can vary dramatically. I buy *creuses*, excellent ones, from the producer's stall at Bouzigues (on the Étang de Thau) for 10 francs the kilo, and a kilo means ten whoppers or eighteen little ones. In a touristic part of Sète, a few miles away, medium-sized ones were 20 francs the dozen. In a restaurant you pay a good deal more (they are nicely served, freshly opened of course, with lemon and bread – often special – and butter), but some five-course 60-franc menus open with half a dozen *creuses*, when the *restaurateur* has made an advantageous purchase.

Oysters are perfectly good in the months with an r; the prejudice against eating them in the summer probably arose through transport problems in hot weather. They are slightly whiter and fatter in the summer, because it is their breeding time.

I cannot do better than quote Alan Davidson:

> *Lavish your money on these delectable creatures, open them, cool them on a bed of ice and, having sprinkled lemon juice, go to it. It is possible to do other things, such as frying or even grilling them,*

not to mention including them in steak and kidney pies, but in my belief they are best eaten as they are, and to do otherwise is mistaken and even blameworthy.

One can even do without the bed of (crushed) ice. But one cannot eat oysters without opening them, and I admire Mr Davidson's coyness here. An expert seems to flip the top shell off with a flick of the knife, but it must have taken me 200 oysters to get from an average of three minutes per oyster to my present 15 seconds. The best advice I can give is: buy some small *creuses* from a friendly merchant and let him give you a lesson, eating as you go. Otherwise, take a small, sharp-pointed knife and hold it so that only half an inch of the pointed end projects from your grip, and carefully, without dangerous strain, work that point in anywhere where you can see the two halves meeting, preferably on the straighter edge, about two-thirds of the distance from the pointed end to the rounded end. Once you have got the point in, change your grip and waggle the blade of the knife so as to cut the muscle where it is attached to the top, flat, shell. If you cannot manage to get the knife in at all, crumble a bit of shell away somewhere with kitchen scissors or a stout knife until a gap is revealed. Like many of the best things in life, it takes a little practice, but I don't think anybody has ever regretted learning how to open an oyster.

If the oyster doesn't care whether it is open or shut, throw it away without bothering to sniff it. Oysters must be alive, and they can live for three or four days out of water, especially if stored round side down in a cool place.

There are other shellfish in the market: various kinds of cockles and clams and winkles; the *escargot de mer, murex brandaris*; sea-urchins (*l'oursin*, m.) which are good but hell to prepare (you eat only the orange ovaries at the bottom). Order a *plateau de fruits de mer* at a good restaurant. It will not be cheap, but two people (or more) can spend a joyous fiddly hour nibbling at such a dish: nicely prepared, it is a gorgeous sight, and the staff will gladly give you the names of all the creatures. But the oysters will be the best of the bunch.

Mussels (*les moules*, f.) – Mediterranean ones can be salty. For *moules marinière* it is sometimes better to throw away part of their liquid, adding the wine later.

Le crabe is the little green crab, used for fish soup. The crab Britons are used to is *le tourteau*.

Le bureau de poste (les PTT) – *the post office*

I love my little local post office. Monsieur Cros, who runs it (his wife does the delivery round in the morning) takes a friendly interest in my affairs, finds attractive big stamps when I write to America and bits of string when he doesn't think my parcels are ship-shape, and gives me all sorts of hints and tips (where to buy car batteries at a discount as well as how to get the best out of the postal services). At the moment he is disappointed in me: I posted a 30-gram letter to London, costing F5,30, and he pointed out that up to 20 grams it's F2,50, so that if I had made it into *two* letters it would have cost me only a total of F5,00. Even allowing five centimes for the extra envelope I would save 25 centimes. But I carry on posting articles to papers in one thrilling instalment, and blow the expense. He feels I am not *sérieux*. . . . Still, I enjoy a chat, and I often make an excuse to call in, such as handing a letter across the counter personally instead of just putting it in the box.

But I will do almost anything to avoid big post offices. I advise you to do the same. Stamps can be bought at the *tabac* (the cigarette shop with the 'carrot' sign outside) within reason. That is to say, they get almost no percentage on selling stamps, so buy something else as well. In villages and small towns the *tabac* usually is a *tabac-journaux*, selling newspapers and postcards; sometimes it's a café too.

One visit to a post office had better be made, however. The people at the *tabac* are not likely to be up to date with postal charges for abroad. You can find these out at a small post office, and even pick up the list of *Principaux Tarifs Postaux*, but a big one might also have the useful *PTT* brochure *'Bienvenue en France'* ('Welcome to France', *'Willkommen in Frankreich'*, etc.) in six languages, with useful information. At many big post offices you can change foreign currency, but a bank is nicer.

If you know what town you're going to, but don't know what your address will be, you can have your mail sent 'Poste restante'. To collect it, you will have to pay a small charge per item, and produce *une pièce d'identité*; this, since Britons refuse to be slaves or have identity cards, will be your passport or similar evidence of identity with a photograph on it. I suppose everyone who writes about this sort of thing says that if your envelope says 'J. Smith Esq' it will probably be filed under E, but it might as well be said again. If the post office person refuses to give it to you, on the grounds that your *pièce d'identité* says your name is Smith, not Esq, just make a fuss in any language; someone in the office will be found to have heard of this British peculiarity.

> postage stamp – *le timbre post*
> parcel – *le paquet*
> registered – *recommandé*
> which is the counter for ——? – *quel est le guichet pour ——?*
> to send a telegram – *expédier un télégramme*
> stop queue-barging – *pardon, monsieur, je crois que c'est mon tour.*

La quincaillerie – *the ironmonger's*

The goods sold by a British ironmonger tend to be split between *la droguerie* and *la quincaillerie*, the latter mainly dealing in metallic objects. Nuts and bolts, power-drills, kitchen scales, cooks' knives and those good cheap Opinel carbon-steel, wood-handled clasp knives; and hinged wire grid-irons that hold steak or sardines firmly, so that you can turn them over on the barbecue without touching them.

La rôtisserie – *the take-away*

I'm not happy about calling it the take-away. A really good *rôtisserie* sells expertly cooked dishes that no French home cook would be ashamed of serving to guests. Generalisation is of course impossible. Treat it as an exhibition. Ask *Qu'est-ce que c'est?* Remember that if you ask for *une portion pour deux* you will get enough for two hearty French eaters who have been up since six in the morning, plus a fair bit extra for seconds; and that if you are camping economically, a whole week's housekeeping can disappear amid the temptations. . . . Still, it's better than losing it at Monte Carlo.

Le tabac – *the tobacconist's*

Le tabac is often combined with other things; some are cafés, and most sell postcards, newspapers and magazines. Frenchmen buy State lottery tickets here, and car licences. Postage stamps, too, which can save queueing at the post office. It is the only place to buy matches (*des allumettes*).

Cigarettes are sold by *le paquet*, holding twenty, and by *la cartouche*, holding ten packets. The authentic Gauloises, smoked by British Francophiles, are the cheapest, and once you get used to them nothing else will do. Gauloises *filtres* have filter tips. Gauloises *sans filtres* let little bits of tobacco get into the mouth. The picturesque yellow kind are Gauloises *papier maïs* (pronounced roughly my-eece); the paper is made of maize leaves, and the cigarette goes out when you put it down.

Voltigeurs are cheap mephitic cigars made, like Gauloises, of French tobacco. When you've had a Voltigeur you know you've had a smoke, and scared the insects away into the bargain.

Cigarettes of Virginia (and Virginia-type) tobacco are on sale too, at prices almost approaching British ones; and real Havana cigars.

The *tabac* is identified by its red *carotte* sign outside.

For women

Sophie tells me that you should have brought with you your kit of preferred products. Here are her tips in case of emergency.

The most expensive source of make-up, etc., is *la parfumerie*, which stocks much more than perfume. Next comes *la pharmacie*. Cheapest is the appropriate section of hypermarket and supermarket, and of some *drogueries*. Alas, there is no Boots.

If money is no object, you will probably find your favourite stuff under the same name, at the *parfumerie*. Otherwise, look for the Mixa-Bébé or Nivea range in the supermarket. These brands have a range of skin tonic (*eau de toilette*) with and without alcohol (*avec/sans alcool*), cleansing milk (*lait de toilette*) and moisturiser (*crème hydratante*).

As for make-up, foundation cream is *le fond de teint*. Lipstick (*le rouge à lèvres*), eye make-up (*le fard à paupières*, *paupières* being eyelids) and nail varnish (*le vernis à ongles*) are displayed and therefore obvious.

Mixa-Bébé and Palmolive are good brands of shampoo (*le shampooing*) and talcum powder (*le talc de toilette*).

The cheaper deodorants and anti-perspirants (same words in French) oddly enough tend to smell powerfully. Revlon Hi-Dri is good.

Cotton wool, *le coton hydrophile*, is cheapest at the super-market.

Tights are *des collants* (m.).

For suntan lotion (*l'huile solaire*, f., e.g. Ambre Solaire) the *pharmacie* might be best; one should certainly go there and ask what they suggest if one has a nasty case of sunburn.

Hydrogen peroxide is *l'eau oxygénée*, also from *la pharmacie*. It comes in three strengths: *dix volumes*, *vingt volumes* and *trente volumes*. The last, 30°, is of course dangerously corrosive, for careful use on incipient moustaches, etc. The 10° is the sort to use as an antiseptic.

Oddments like nail-brushes, nail-files, combs, etc., are easily

157

identifiable in transparent plastic packs in the supermarket. Sanitary towels can come from there, too: *serviettes hygiéniques*. Little pads are *protège-slips*. Tampax is Tampax.

If consulting the doctor, periods are *les règles*. 'I am (—— months) pregnant' – *Je suis enceinte (de —— mois)*.

Chapter 15

The telephone

All telephone numbers in France have eight figures. If the number you want to phone seems to have six figures, or seven, you are using pre-October 1985 information. Don't despair: see below for the earlier method and how to use it.

Making calls within France: telephonically, France is divided into two parts. One part is the Paris region. The other part is all the rest of the country. The telephone people call the first part *Paris/Région Parisienne* and the second part *Province* (meaning 'the provinces') and I wish they wouldn't, because of Provence, with an 'e', which isn't a telephonic region. But I had better use the *PTT*'s terms.

If you are in France and want to phone someone in the same telephonic part of France, just dial the eight figures.

If you are in *Paris/Région Parisienne* and you want to phone *Province*, dial 16. Wait for a new 'tone' (it will probably come at once) and then dial the eight figures. The numbers 16 mean 'Get me out of *Paris/Région Parisienne* and into the rest of the country.'

If you are in *Province* and you want to phone *Paris/Région Parisienne*, dial 16, wait for a new 'tone', then dial 1, and then dial the eight figures. Dialling 16-(tone)-1 means 'Get me out of the provinces and into *Paris/Région Parisienne.*'

Ringing the UK from France: First dial 19, to go international. Wait for a new dialling tone (it often comes at once). Then dial 44 (for the UK), immediately followed by the British STD code *omitting the zero*, and the number. Rapid pip-pip-pip noises mean 'We're working on it', or you may hear nothing for several seconds – don't hang up, they're still working on it.

If you are phoning abroad from France and after dialling you hear someone talking French (and if you can't understand it), you are probably listening to a recorded message saying that all the lines out of France are engaged, and would you please try later ... Try again at once, and then if you haven't got through, believe them. Or the message may be saying there's no such number; don't believe them: try again, having checked whether you have mis-dialled (a frequent mistake is including the 0 with British numbers).

Directory enquiries for French numbers: dial 12 (you have to pay for the call). There may be the sound of music and a pre-recorded voice saying, in effect, 'Hang on, we're busy'.

Directory enquiries for UK numbers: first dial 19; wait for new dialling tone, as above; then dial 33 (enquiries) and 44 (UK).

Reversed-charge calls for French numbers: dial 10; you want to make *une communication en PCV* (pay-say-vay). But they are thinking of abolishing this service, and may already have done so when you need it.

Reversed-charge calls for UK numbers (*not* due for abolition): dial as for directory enquiries about UK numbers, and go ahead in English or French. The process can take ages, as there are not many operators these days. It is quicker (and cheaper for the person you want to talk to) to make a very short direct call, costing only a couple of francs, and ask to be phoned back.

Police: dial 17.

Telephone directories: each *département* has its directory (*une annuaire*). Numbers are listed under *communes*. All the place-names beginning *Sainte* come after all those beginning *Saint*.

In a hotel bedroom you may be able to dial direct, or your call may have to go through the receptionist. (The Michelin guide's symbols for the hotel say which applies.) To dictate a telephone number, see page 201. If baffled, you will have to write it down and give it to the receptionist. The hotel is allowed to make an extra charge on top of the cost of the call.

There is more than one type of public telephone booth in action; 'improvements' are mainly designed to frustrate thieves and vandals. Booths work more or less as in Britain, and international calls can be made from them.

The cost goes up with a sharp bump (at the time of writing) when calls are made to outside the immediate neighbourhood, and then flattens out with further distance. Per price-unit, I get unlimited time on a local call, but only 12 seconds for somewhere 40 or 400 miles away; I get 11 seconds for anywhere in Great Britain. That is at the full rate. The *PTT* keep changing their minds about prices for times of day. As I write, there is a 65 per cent reduction between 11 p.m. and 6 a.m., with 50 per cent and 30 per cent reductions at other times, and reductions on Saturday afternoons and Sundays. That is for France-to-France calls. For phoning the UK from France, there are 15 seconds per unit instead of 11 from 9.30 p.m. to 8 a.m. (French time); from 2 p.m. on Saturdays and all day Sundays and on French public holidays. When phoning the USA and Canada, the reduction period is from 10 p.m. to 10 a.m. French time, and all day on Sundays and French public holidays. However, as I have said, there is a fair amount of chopping and changing about the price of calls, and anybody seriously interested in getting the maximum for his money should consult a current French phone directory (*l'annuaire*).

the telephone – *le téléphone*
the telephone booth – *la cabine téléphonique*

a phone call – (in written-style French) *une communication téléphonique;* (otherwise) *un coup de téléphone*

I want to make a call to —— – *Je voudrais téléphoner à* ——

Hallo – *Allo*

Hang on! – *Ne quittez pas!*

How to say phone numbers in French: see page 201

The pre-October 1985 system: and how to convert from it

Before 25 October 1985, instead of two zones there were 64. Everybody had either a six-figure number or a seven-figure number. Their zone had a prefix; this was two figures if they had a six-figure number, or one figure if they had a seven-figure number. The prefix was usually indicated in brackets before the six- or seven-figure number. To phone someone in the same zone, you just dialled the six or seven figures; to get out of the zone, you dialled 16, then the prefix, then the rest.

In October 1985 the prefix was incorporated into the number, giving the present eight-figure numbers. (The town of Paris itself and the immediately neighbouring *départements,* but not the rest of the present *Paris/Région Parisienne* part, had the prefix 1; at the October change this became 4. That was the only exception.)

The Hotel Negresco at Nice stated its number as (93) 88 39 51. It now states it as 93 88 39 51. No problem. The Michelin guide just gave it as 88 39 51; you had to look at the beginning of the Nice section to learn that the prefix was 93. If you have an old Michelin you can still do that; the only difference being that you now include the prefix even if you're phoning from the café round the corner.

The Ritz in Paris gave its number as (1) 260 38 30. Aha, a trap here; but you now know that the 1 prefix became a 4 at the October change in 1985. So the present number is 42 60 38 30.

The telephonic alphabet

What follows is a routine alphabet for spelling words over the phone. But it should be used only if one can say the alphabet in French (see page 200) and make a reasonable stab at pronouncing the names, otherwise confusion will be worse confounded.

A pour Anatole
B pour Berthe
C pour Camille
D pour Désiré
E pour Eugène
F pour François
G pour Gaston
H pour Henri
I pour Irma
J pour Jean
K pour Kléber
L pour Louis
M pour Marcel
N pour Noémie
O pour Oscar
P pour Pierre
Q pour Quintal
R pour Roger
S pour Suzanne
T pour Thérèse
U pour Ursule
V pour Victor
W pour William
X pour Xavier
Y pour Yvonne
Z pour Zoé

Chapter 16

Children

The French are, on average, more indulgent towards children than the British. This indulgence takes the form of treating them as adults, more or less, except when they make themselves a nuisance. Thus, while British parents might painstakingly pander to their children during the day, and then pack them off to bed with a cry of relief, French children (on holiday) stay up till all hours so long as they don't interfere with adult activities. Similarly at meal-times – especially at restaurants – they are expected to behave in an adult fashion through the long eating ritual, and a large proportion of them succeed, to their own apparent satisfaction. Tiny tots are usually greeted with enthusiasm. One need have few qualms about a welcome for British children when travelling. Self-catering in *gîte* or tent is of course the cheapest way of feeding them (on favourite tins brought from home?) and if they are hide-bound traditionalists such a régime is easier too; but if they are adventurous, inquisitive and open-minded they will enjoy hotels and restaurants in France.

For small children, some hotel and restaurant keepers have

signed a 'children's charter': they exhibit a cheerful sign showing two tots and a baby, and guarantee certain facilities: a feeding-bottle warmer (*un chauffe-biberon*), proprietary infant food in little pots, high chairs (*une chaise-bébé*) and so forth. But absence of that sign does *not* mean that such facilities are not available. Even supermarket cafeterias have high chairs. Most hotels will put a cot (*un lit d'enfant*) in a double room, at an extra charge (free sometimes).

At restaurants, there is sometimes a children's menu (*un menu d'enfant*), but that is not part of the traditional way of life. If a child is too small to attempt the adult menu, the usual French practice is to ask for *un couvert* (plate, cutlery); the child then gets served from the parents' portions. Sometimes a small charge is made for a *couvert*, sometimes none. This facility should be approached with discretion; one 'free' child per two paying parents is fine, but if you are a couple with four children you can hardly expect to be allowed to feed your offspring from the surplus of two menus. Four menus and two *couverts* would be acceptable. There is usually something *à la carte* that will do; *du poulet froid avec des frites* (cold chicken and chips) can usually be rustled up even if it isn't on the menu.

School: if you are in France during term-time, state schools will accept your children, free, if there is room.

Chapter 17

The doctor

Language first. The doctor is *le médecin*, whether male (and addressed as *Monsieur le docteur*) or female (and addressed as *Madame le docteur*). The profession he or she practises is *la médecine*. The drugs on his or her *ordonnance* (f., prescription) are *médicaments* (m.).

First, the good news. Doctors are, in general, as highly qualified as in Britain – if not more highly. And they are glad to see you, because there are a lot more of them than in Britain, and it is a piece-rate job. Not only that, but they are happy to pay home visits; it makes a change from seeing patients in the consulting room, and the fee is higher.

See the section on the chemist (page 147) for some basic advice and vocabulary. While a visit to the chemist might present some language problems, there should be little trouble with the doctor. He knows some English, and anyway he is skilled in diagnosis; human bodies are the same on both sides of the Channel; babies who can't speak and people who are unconscious are treated successfully. For this reason I have resisted the temptation to fill a couple of pages with labelled anatomical diagrams and names of diseases and lesions. If the doctor prods you in the appendix region and says *Cela vous fait mal?* ('Does that hurt?') it won't matter whether you say 'Ouch!' or 'Aïe!'

However, if you suffer from some long-standing complaint which might cause trouble while you are in France, it would help if you could persuade your overworked British doctor to get his secretary to type out a short statement of the case. Written English is easier, for your French doctor, than spoken English; he probably reads some medical literature in English (reports of international conferences, for example). Similarly, if in Britain you are frequently prescribed a prescription drug, and you think you might need a further supply, it could help to take an old empty packet along. Some 'patent' drugs – Tagamet, Valium and Mogadon, for example – have the same brand-name on both sides of the Channel, because they are made by international pharmaceutical giants, but others have different brand-names; a glance at the packet will show the doctor what the real name of the active ingredient is (it is often a colossal word of fifteen syllables, unpronounceable in any language) and he will know its French brand-name.

One or two words, nevertheless. *L'intoxication* (f.) is food-poisoning, not drunkenness (which is *l'ivresse*, f.); do not take umbrage if the doctor says you are *intoxiqué*. 'I am allergic to ——' – *Je suis allergique au/à la/aux* ——. This is more medical than *Je ne supporte pas le/la/les* ——. See remarks on suppositories on page 148. While we are on that subject, the standard French thermometer is a rectal one, and some people prefer to bring their own British thermometer, the kind you stick in your mouth instead. If you are two degrees 'up', in fahrenheit, you are roughly one degree 'up' in centigrade, and can tell the doctor *j'ai un degré de fièvre* instead of letting him find out himself. (He has heard about British squeamishness in this matter, though he might have classified the notion with British tales of the French living on frogs and snails, or French stories that the British undertake sexual intercourse only as a patriotic duty.)

At the drop of a hat he will take your *tension* (f.), blood pressure. Your blood group is your *groupe sanguin* (m.), and he might take *une prise de sang* (a blood sample) for testing. *Une piqûre* – an injection. *Une radio(graphie)* – an X-ray.

Un généraliste, a general practitioner, is probably the person you will want to see. But nothing prevents your consulting *un spécialiste* direct; they will be found in the telephone directory, yellow pages, under the heading *médecins: généralistes* first, then *spécialistes* under their speciality. They cost more.

Dog bites, and bites and scratches from other animals can be dangerous: there is rabies (*la rage*) on the continent. See a doctor at once. A gratifying amount of nuisance will be caused to the animal's owner: the beast is not allowed a 'free' first bite as in Britain, and it will need a rabies test at the vet's.

At the time of writing there is no '999 – ambulance' call in France, though something similar is planned. But of course there are emergency services, and any local will ring the appropriate number for his district. The number for the police is 17; they have a *secours* (emergency rescue) service. For less urgent matters, if you don't want to roam around looking for a doctor's brass plate, *la pharmacie*, a neighbour, the hotel-keeper or someone at the campsite office will know about local doctors.

And now the bad news (not very bad, really). The French National Health Service works by having everybody (and their employers) make contributions to one of a number of organisations connected with their trade or profession. The patient pays cash when he consults his doctor and when he gets his stuff from the chemist. Then, *on production of a contribution certificate* and not otherwise, he gets about three-quarters of the cost back (more, or all, in the case of major trouble) from the local office for repayment: *la caisse primaire d'assurance maladie*. Your certificate is the Form E 111 which you will have obtained from your nearest Department of Health and Social Security office before you left home; a valuable document.

To get repayment, you and the French have to do some

paperwork. If you have taken out a holiday insurance policy with a private company in England, it might not be worth bothering to use your Form E 111 and go through all the red tape. My own view is that one should have an inexpensive 'holiday' policy, to deal with minor matters (don't forget to get a receipt from doctor and chemist) *and* to cover return to Britain by ambulance if necessary; but one should also have the Form E 111, since with that the sky's the limit and there are no exclusions (such as pre-existing defects, pregnancy and other things in the small print of private policies).

Using the Form E 111 you are just like a Frenchperson. Don't forget to pay the doctor! Some British people are so used to seeing doctors 'free' that they wander out of the surgery without paying; and – despite allegations of avarice – I have consulted two doctors who were too nice to bring up the sordid subject; the result being that I had to double back when I realised. . . .

So you will pay (*C'est combien?* – it is around £7.00 at the surgery for a GP in 1986, more for a home visit) and you will ask for *une feuille de maladie*, an important form, part of which the doctor will fill in for you. There are just a few doctors who are not in the 'national health' service, that is who are *non-conventionné*, but it is unlikely that you would meet such elegant creatures unless you are ill in the Ritz and fail to mention that you want *un médecin conventionné*, the sort who has *feuilles de maladie* like the vast majority of the profession.

Go to *la pharmacie* (see page 147) with your *ordonnance* and your *feuille de maladie*. Pay for your *médicaments*, bandages and whatnot. On each box or bottle there is a sticky label, *la vignette*, identifying the item and showing its price. The *pharmacien* or you will stick those labels on the *feuille de maladie*. Now ask the chemist for the address of the regional *caisse primaire*, and write it down.

Your next job is to send your *feuille de maladie* (after completing your part of it – not difficult, and everybody in France knows the form) AND your *ordonnance* (important, to prove that the doctor really did prescribe the stuff) AND your

Form E 111 to that *caisse primaire*. But wait! Are you sure that you are now cured and are going to be fighting fit until you see the white cliffs of Dover – and that none of your dependants named on the E 111 will need any medical treatment? No? Then wait, because once you have fired off your E 111 there are no more shots in your locker. Further treatment for the same complaint, and further *vignettes*, can go on the same *feuille de maladie*, or you could have a fresh one, and on a really unlucky holiday you might collect *feuilles* and *ordonnances* for all the family. Your E 111 goes in with your total claim.

You can perfectly well wait until you are back home in the overcrowded arms of the NHS before posting off the whole bundle of bumf to the appropriate *caisse primaire* whose address you have carefully noted. (If you want to count every penny, such mail goes free in France: you write *dispense d'affranchisse-ment – sécurité sociale* at the top of the envelope, post it just before you board the boat, and save a stamp.)

Then, a couple of months later, a money order will arrive at your home address, the one you wrote on your *feuille de maladie,* repaying about three-quarters of your outlay.

Something really nasty, for which you get taken to hospital, might turn out to be free, or nearly, but you will still need your E 111. In case of bureaucratic or financial crisis the nearest British Consul should be contacted (see page 176). He has no funds to bail you out, but he is skilled at finding solutions for people in serious difficulty.

The main ailments among British holidaymakers down here are caused by getting bloated with too much good food, fuddled by too much cheap wine and then lying around in the midday sun, but you are not like that. Oh yes, there's *l'hydrocution*: loss of consciousness or death through sudden immersion in water, when one is too hot. Take it easy.

Chapter 18

The British Consul

Let us hope you never need him.

He has a job to do, and does it well. The occasions when you might call for his help are mainly those where the routine is familiar to him but bewilderingly new for you, such as:

- Death: if you should die in France, the Consul will be in his element. He will deal with the local red tape, arrange for next of kin to be informed, and advise on procedures.
- Prison: he will come and see you if you ask, and provide a list of local lawyers. But he cannot get you out, get you better treatment than similar French prisoners, or give you legal advice himself.
- Hospital: if you are taken to hospital he can arrange for next of kin to be informed; and if, through some ghastly oversight, you are not adequately insured, he will advise you on how to transfer your own funds, and even arrange for your friends and relations to be contacted, so that they can stump up for your medical bills and your ticket home.
- Theft: if everything you have is stolen, he will issue an emergency passport to get you home, and (as in the

hospital situation) will advise you on how to transfer your funds, or those of your friends or relations. But he cannot investigate the crime himself, or give you legal advice.

- Neediness: it should be taken as a principle that the Consul has *no money*. But see hospital and theft, above. Hard luck stories from lame ducks who spend all their cash making whoopee on the way down to the Mediterranean shore, and think that someone should fork out to get them back home, are less successful with Her Majesty's consular staff than with sentimental French police inspectors and golden-hearted chuckers-out at brothels. The Consul cannot provide a list of such potential benefactors. But it is better to approach him than to commit suicide or crime, if stranded. Something might be done, but it is most unlikely to take the form of handing over spendable francs.

A Consul is a full-time official. An Honorary Consul is someone who has another job, which naturally has first call on his time. If he is not available, call the nearest Consulate General. For addresses see page 208.

Chapter 19

Wine

Making wine is easy. Just crush some grapes. Very soon little bubbles begin to rise to the surface of the mush. This is because the micro-organisms (yeasts) on the grape-skins have begun to multiply, changing the grape-sugar into gas and alcohol.

After a few days the bubbling stops. The gas has drifted away with a cheerful smell of fermentation, and all the sugar has been converted. The liquid contains 9–14 per cent of alcohol, depending on how sweet the grapes were. Strain off the solids (skins, pips, perhaps a few stalks) and there's your wine. Keep the air out or it will turn to vinegar.

That's red wine. For white wine, you just ferment the juice without the skins. (White wine is usually made from the juice of black grapes; if white grapes are used it is called *blanc de blancs*.)

For *rosé* wine leave the skins in for a short while.

For fizzy wine, bottle the wine with a small shot of sugar syrup, and hope that the remaining yeasts will start it fermenting again – enough to produce a loud pop when you remove the wired-on cork, but not enough to make the bottle explode in the cellar.

Pasteur called wine 'the healthiest and most hygienic of all drinks', as wine-growers in the south of France keep reminding us on their posters. What Pasteur was really saying was that water, in his day, was a risky sort of drink. Alcohol is an antiseptic, and wine is safe. Pasteur was thinking about cholera and so forth, not about drunken drivers or the fact that if one drinks much more than a litre of wine a day, seven days a week, for thirty or forty years, one may get cirrhosis of the liver.

No wonder that the first thing Noah did when he got out of the ark and sent those smelly animals on their way was to plant a vineyard and praise the Lord for landing him in the right climate. Wine is mankind's oldest drink, apart from all that water. It is good for you, both physically (valuable minerals and trace elements) and spiritually (wine people are nice people; beware of alcoholics hooked on spirits, rampaging beer-guzzlers and fanatical teetotallers). Not more than a litre a day, remember, or to be on the safe side, say, 300 litres a year, or 400 standard 75cl wine-bottles: a bottle a day and two on Sundays. But if you take any other alcoholic drinks at all, you must reduce the wine ration, alas, to keep in first-class shape.

Cheap, too. My neighbour Henri makes a fair living out of his 15 hectares (about 37 acres) of vineyards. He does all the work himself, with the aid of a tractor, except for three weeks' grape-picking, when he hires a family of Spaniards and a British student or two. In an average year he gets about 8000 litres per hectare, or 3250 litres per acre. So his 15 hectares produce about 120,000 litres; enough for 160,000 wine-bottles. If you take your jerrycans down to the winery you can buy it from the pump at 4 francs the litre. It isn't cheap plonk to fill the EEC wine lake, but good wine that I'm glad to have. I bottle it myself when I get home from the winery, and I like to keep a couple of hundred bottles in the cellar, just in case next year is a poor year. So each 75cl bottle costs me under 30p. Like Omar Khayyám, 'I often wonder what the Vintners buy /

One half so precious as the Goods they sell'. . .

On the other hand, there is Château Whatsit 1961, for which sane men in England – and in France too – are glad to pay £100 a bottle when they can track one down. Basically, it's the same as Henri's. The varieties of vine needed to produce this wine are not so productive, and the soil in which they grow doesn't look up to much: thin stony stuff. Nothing like 8000 litres per hectare. Château Whatsit is further north, and the grapes ripen more slowly. When the wine is made it tastes harsh. Centuries ago people learnt that if you take carefully made wine from these small vineyards, mostly around Bordeaux, and keep it even more carefully for anything from a decade to a quarter of a century, then – with luck as well as care – a sip, taken gently and rolled around the mouth and aerated with little gulps of air, can make you feel like falling on your knees in wonder, and crying for joy. It isn't the alcohol, good heavens! – Henri's wine is a bit stronger. Nobody knows exactly what combination of factors (something in the soil? the weather that year?) makes the difference.

Henri's wine is drunk the year after it's made. A further year might make it a little smoother, but after that it begins to lose some of its modest quality. So Henri will not be tempted to keep his 1986 vintage until AD 2000 before selling it – and anyway he couldn't afford to lock his capital up like that.

In between Henri's wine and Château Whatsit is a bewildering range, but most of the eighty thousand million litres that France makes in a good year are like Henri's: an honest beverage tasting of grapes and sunshine, but without anything like the bouquet and finesse of Château Whatsit 1961 drunk in 1986. Below Henri's there's still a certain amount of nasty thin stuff made on rich soil from grapes that squirt masses of tasteless juice. There remain about ten per cent of superior wines, among which Château Whatsit and its equals amount to a minuscule fraction.

Let us now begin to come to the practical point. Two points, really: one about buying wine in England and a quite different one about buying it in France.

As I was saying, when I take my jerrycans to the filling-station, Henri's wine costs me 4 francs the litre. Henri's *cave coopérative* also puts it up in litre bottles, corked and labelled: between 6 and 7 francs the litre, depending on where you buy it, with a franc deposit on the bottle. They also present it in standard non-returnable 75cl wine-bottles, elegantly labelled. These bottles of wine cost 7 francs each; 3 francs' worth (three-quarters of a litre) of pump-price wine.

In England they cost £2 each, for the same 3 francs' worth. ... The excise duty takes the biggest bite. As the British importer takes it away from the *cave coopérative* in big wine tankers, at a discount, instead of in ten-litre containers, it's an exaggeration to say that the bottle holds 3 francs' worth.

If I drive 15 miles I can get some noticeably superior wine (an *appellation contrôlée*). It would perhaps cost me twice as much as Henri's – say, 8 francs the litre – if they would sell it to me from the pump, but they won't do that for small customers. I have to pay 12 francs for the 75cl bottle, therefore. That works out at 16 francs the litre, or four times dearer than my daily table wine. But the British merchant buys it in bulk. The duty, transport and bottling costs are the same as with Henri's wine. The wine in your bottle in England is worth twice as much; you pay £2.25 instead of £2. ...

And when we move further up-market, we find that for £10 we can get as good a bottle of wine in England as in France, with luck, and for £25 a better one. The British exciseman makes no distinction between Château Whatsit and the poorest plonk, and at the expensive end of the range other sorts of taxation bite more deeply in France.

The moral is clear. In England one should drink the better wines, even if that means having to share a weekly or alas! fortnightly bottle. When one crosses the Channel, one should not expect to get a bottle like that for less than half-price, but one can give three resounding cheers for wine like Henri's – decent honest wine for drinking with every meal, and cooking with, with one's mind financially at rest.

Wine in restaurants

In restaurants that have no *bc* and no carafe symbol in the Michelin guide, one chooses one's wine from the *carte des vins*, paying upwards of 35 francs for wine that is often no better than carafe or 'free' wine. One should not get irritated about this, as long as one knows in advance. The restaurants concerned are often more elegant than others, or in a better situation, and their menus may be competitively generous; they hope to make their main profit on the wine. If one is hard up, and there is no mention on the menu outside of *vin en pichet* or *vin compris*, then to avoid embarrassment it is safer to assume that the cheapest wine will be 45 francs for a normal 75cl bottle, and that it will not be available in half-bottles; and re-calculate the cost of a meal accordingly before entering. But it is always worth asking: *avez-vous du vin en carafe?*

Of course, in all restaurants superior wines can be ordered from the *carte des vins*. The price will be about three times the 'shop' price. This seems outrageous; restaurateurs explain that it is inevitable, given the way their tax inspector works. He is wary of taking their word as to their annual takings; instead, he looks at the bills for products coming into the establishment, multiplies the figure by three and assumes that that was what the customers' bills came to. This seems fair enough, as far as the food is concerned, when one considers all the work involved, and the overheads – and indeed, when my wife and I try to cost some of the excellent meals we have in average French restaurants, we are amazed that they can do it at the price. But as for wine – well, when we feel like a moderately expensive meal, elegantly served on a shady terrace overlooking the sea, we don't grudge the mark-up on the modest bottle we share. But as for really fine wines, we keep them for celebrations at home.

Then there are the restaurants with two or three stars in Michelin, or three or four *toques* in Gault Millau. Most of these have excellent cellars, carefully looked after by attentive *sommeliers* (wine waiters) who are ready to give sound advice on what to drink with what – or, perhaps more appropriately if one is going to pay a company director's ransom for a bottle, what to eat with what. If one has gone there mainly for the food, or for the luxurious surroundings, napery, service and whatnot, one will do quite well to choose the least expensive wine on the list. (Some shy people always choose the least-expensive-but-one.) It will not be cheap, but it will be good enough. Be reassured by *The Official Foodie Handbook:* 'In France, Foodies order the local wine. You do not want the claims of a great vintage to get in the way of the claims of a great chef. And anyway, if God had not intended the local wine to be drunk with the menu, He would not have placed the restaurant there.' It is irrational to pay 600 francs in one of these places for a bottle that one can buy for 200 francs outside, but if one is in a temple of gastronomy and paying some 300 francs a head for dinner, it is a minor affair to pay 80 francs for a bottle worth 25 francs; and it will be good wine, probably from a local vineyard.

On the other hand, it is possible that the restaurateur has cornered the only stocks of the wine he's selling at 600 francs. He may have laid the bottles down years ago, and now they are just right, worthy of the profoundest worship, and you can't get them outside for love nor money. Well, if that is what you want, do please take the trouble to order your meal and your precious bottle the day before. The *sommelier* will then be able to stand the bottle upright for 24 hours at the right temperature, and you may be regarded not only as a good customer but also as a worthy one.

Wine in hotels

The situation is of course the same as with restaurants. People holidaying on a tight budget, who want to stay put on *pension* terms in one hotel for a while and who do not want to grieve over the cost of wine with their meals, should take into consideration the system prevailing in the hotels they might choose. Two hotels might seem to charge the same *pension* terms for room and all meals; but if in one of them the wine is free, or available *en carafe*, and if the other charges a steepish price per bottle, the difference in total cost can be considerable, on the basis of half a bottle per meal per person.

If the hotels are in the Michelin guide, one can do one's research on this matter before leaving England by seeing whether the hotels have *bc* or carafe indications.

Wine in cafés

Many English people enjoy drinking a glass of ordinary table wine between meals. Such tipples are nowadays readily sold in English pubs (at English prices). The picture is rather different in French cafés, where you may get a dusty answer if you ask for a simple glass of wine. In humble and obscure cafés *un coup de rouge* (a shot of red) may be served to humble and obscure customers, but it will not be brought to the table on the terrace on the promenade. There, they want to serve you relatively expensive drinks such as beer, *apéritifs*, orangeade or Vichy water.

There are a few wine bars in big cities, where fine vintage wines are served by the glass. And most cafés will happily provide a costly bottle of champagne in an ice bucket, which makes a pleasant round for four or five people, and an even better round for two. Special wines may sometimes be had in their season – the over-publicised Beaujolais *nouveau*, for example. And along the Loire, in November, small cafés sell *bernache* for almost nothing: white wine that is still 'working', cloudy, faintly fizzy and quite delicious.

But the general rule is: table wine is for the dining room, at meal-times; not for the café.

Buying wine

England and Scotland (and perhaps Wales and Ireland, for all I know) have a centuries-old tradition of fine old merchants of fine old wines; and recent evolutions in habits have led big British supermarket chains to track down excellent wines from all over the world and sell them without fuss at competitive prices.

Newcomers to France who expect to find bigger, better and more comprehensive establishments are often disappointed at first. There are very few fine old wine shops for fine old discussions about cobwebbed vintages. (There are some in Paris – two are run by expert Britons.) The French connoisseur buys his finer wines at the place of production. He visits vineyards and wine-makers; he does some canny tasting at wine-fairs and exhibitions; and his *bonnes bouteilles* are delivered by the case. With every middle-class flat in France goes a heavily padlocked section of cellar, for wine to rest in. The wine bought in its harsh ungracious youth matures there for five, ten, fifteen years. . . .

Wine is bought in shops for immediate consumption: the ordinary daily ration, and a better bottle in emergencies. Although France is the top country for wine, both in quality and quantity, the shops hardly reflect that fact. You are likely to find a goodish choice of ordinary and somewhat-above-ordinary wines, and a modest selection of more expensive ones; and of course champagne, which is usually bought as and when needed. You'll find very few 'foreign' wines, except port, which some misguided French people drink as an *apéritif.* Sherry is almost unknown.

In my village (eighty inhabitants, no shops) the travelling grocer stops in the square every Tuesday and Saturday, bringing all kinds of things – even Vichy and Evian water – but no wine. The summer holiday-makers and winter sabbatical-leave scholars who rent *gîtes* buy their wine, at first, from the supermarket four miles away. Then they learn to make pleasant excursions to some of the many vineyards, *caves coopératives* and *domaines* within an hour's drive. They do some free tasting (*dégustation gratuite* say the notices) and become knowledgeable about the local products, ranging from *vin de pays* through *VDQS* to *AOC* (see page 182); grape varieties ('ten per cent Cabernet Sauvignon and twenty per cent Syrah . . .') ~nd soil ('it's grown on the schist . . .'). They buy by the bottle or by the jerrican, have a splendid time, and all at between a fifth and a half of British prices.

In other words: for buying Château Whatsit 1961 and its equals, London is as good as Paris and better than Avignon or Antibes. But for the other 99 per cent of French wine, France is the place. If you are in a wine region, do some field research and have fun. If you are staying in some other part of France, make wide selections from the available gamut of sound inexpensive bottles, and for every wine that pleases you, note where it came from and plan to call there, one sunny day.

THE LANGUAGE OF WINE-BUYING

At the shop
In the wine section of the *hypermarché, supermarché* and *épicerie* you will see:

vin de table. This is a misleading name. Even Château Whatsit is table wine; that is, you drink it with food. *Vin de table* is the humblest. It may be in throw-away plastic bottles, holding 1, 1½ or 2 litres, or in returnable glass litre bottles with stars embossed near the shoulder (to do with the bottle, not the wine) on which you will be charged a franc or so as deposit; as for the empties, see page 192. If you look at the small print on the label, you may see *vin de plusieurs pays de la CÉE* – a blend of wine from more than one country of the EEC. This will be all right, but nothing to write home about (except the low price). Or it may say *vin de France* or *vin français* – a blend of French wines, not necessarily any better or dearer. Wine of this sort has a mention of the alcoholic strength, probably 10°, 11° or 12°. 'The stronger the better' is a rough guide at this level, on the grounds that the highly productive but undistinguished grapes that make the cheaper wines have most flavour when they have most original sugar. (This is *not* the case with fine wines, which may be light in alcohol but superb; their vines are less productive varieties, the sugar content of the grapes being less important than the aroma and flavours that develop with age, and may be gathered before the sugar content is at its maximum to give a late-developing wine. Such wines do not state their alcohol content on their labels.)

vin de pays. Usually in returnable litres or non-returnable 75cl normal wine-bottles. This label means that the wine is from one named district only, not a blend from several regions. It may be a little dearer than the *vin de table*, depending on the *pays*. It is certainly worth trying a selection, as these wines have individual character, though it would be rash to assert that any one, taken at random, will be certain to please you more than a decent *vin de table*. If you are in a wine region, it is especially worth buying a bottle of each of a number of local *vins de pays*, with a view to calling on the producer of a good one, and buying *en vrac* (see page 185). Henri's wine (page 174) is a *vin de pays*, sold as such under the label of the local *cave coopérative*.

VDQS – vin délimité de qualité supérieure. Normal wine-bottles. The next step up. To carry the *VDQS* mention on its label the wine must fulfil a number of conditions (district, grape varieties, method of pruning; tasting tests . . .) and there is a fair chance that a random *VDQS* will please you more than a random *vin de pays*, so it is worth the extra franc or two to include some of these bottles in your sample. Notice that I say a *fair* chance: the point is that one of the *VDQS* conditions is a restriction on the total output sold under that producer's *VDQS* label (not so much to keep the price up as to remove the temptation to resort to practices that increase output but reduce quality: fertilisers, for example, can lead to lots of juice but not much flavour). Now, in a good year the producer may find he's got too much of this good wine; so the excess, over and above what he is allowed to sell as *VDQS* goes into his *vin de table* vats. . . . *VDQS* may disappear in the future, the wines becoming *vin de pays* or *AOC*.

AOC – appellation d'origine contrôlée. As *VDQS* but better, at least in theory, with strict regulations according to each *appellation*. This is the top category, stretching from middling wines, which might cost as little as two or three times the price of a *vin de pays*, up to the noblest aristocrats. The remarks above, about excess production of *VDQS*, apply also to *AOC*. A few *AOC* wines can be bought *en vrac*, with luck, but producers prefer to sell them in bottles. While a randomly chosen *AOC* is likely to be better than an equally random *VDQS* or *vin de pays*, home wine-tastings sometimes select a non-*AOC* as best of the candidates; in which case, wine being a natural and chancy product, one should get some more of the wine one likes without delay: a later batch (especially when buying *en vrac*, from the pump) may not be the same.

All the above categories of meal-time wine include *vin rouge* (red), *vin blanc* (white) and *vin rosé*, which doesn't seem to have an English name, and occasionally calls itself something odd, such as *vin gris* (grey, but it isn't) and *pelure d'oignon* (onion skin, referring to the colour, not the taste). Sweetish white wines, suitable for the pudding course, will usually have *doux* (sweet) on their label, or *moelleux* (somewhat less sweet), unless they are supposed to be well enough known (Sauternes, for example) for the customer not to need telling. *Brut* is dry.

As for the most prominent word or words on the label, they are of little help to the newcomer experimenting with the bulk of France's wines. (The situation is different with the top one per cent, about which there is an exceedingly copious literature in English already.) There may be a made-up name, a 'brand' (Chantemerle, Duchesse de Machin-Truc, Coeur Charmant . . .), especially in the case of *vins de table* and *vins de pays*; or the name of the district, village or vineyard (Beaujolais, Saint-Saturnin, Clos de Somewhere) and/or of the variety of grape if only one variety is used (Cabernet Sauvignon, Muscadet, Sylvaner). The prettiest labels are the work of marketing experts, not of wine-makers.

vin doux naturel is not a table wine. Despite the name, it is not really *naturel*; it has been interfered with, to the extent of adding some alcohol early in the process. This stops the fermentation, as yeasts give up when the alcohol content rises to something like 15 per cent; thus there is some grape sugar left unchanged, and you have a strongish sweet drink. I rather like a small glassful of Muscat de Frontignan, very occasionally: the soul of the muscat grape. The cost is about five times that of an ordinary wine.

vin mousseux is fizzy wine. Champagne (a district with severe regulations) is an example, costing almost as much as in Britain. Going down-market, one finds other *vins mousseux* made by the champagne method (*méthode champenoise* on the label), which involves doing the secondary fermentation in the bottle and then getting rid of the resulting yeast deposit by a tricky and labour-intensive process. This yields the longest-lasting bubbles, and there is little point in using an inferior wine to start with. Further down-market, there is *mousseux* made *en cuve close*. Here, the secondary fermentation takes place in a closed vat. The yeasts sink to the bottom of the vat, and the wine is bottled off under pressure. Then there is a little *mousseux* made by what might be called the Coca-Cola method – injecting gas; no one would do that to a decent wine.

If you are wealthy you will have your favourite champagne everywhere you go, for elevenses. If less wealthy, I advise you to drink your champagne in Britain; there, the duty is heavy on all sparkling wines, making the non-champagne ones less of a comparative bargain. In France, a non-champagne *vin mousseux, méthode champenoise* can be excellent, at half the price of fizz from Champagne. So can a *cuve close*, at a quarter of the champagne price or less – around the price of beer in Britain. Worth experimenting. Start, perhaps, with Vouvray, or Blanquette de Limoux, or Clairette de Die. They all come in champagne bottles, with champagne corks that go pop.

Port is called *porto*, and comes in many brands, most of them inferior to what one finds in Britain. Sherry, however, is unlikely to be found (they call it *vin de Xérès*). In France one can do very well by sticking to French drinks, except for French whisky (it does exist).

From the producer

Buying direct from the wine-maker, you might perhaps get better wine. If it is in bottle it probably won't be cheaper than at the most competitive shop, but if you buy it *en vrac* (see below) it will cost much less.

More important for most people, buying direct is more fun. Holiday-makers who do their own catering sometimes find that their wine-tasting and wine-buying excursions are among the most interesting and satisfying experiences of their stay, and some of them wisely take home a liquid souvenir that gives them pleasure until Christmas or beyond.

Vente de Vin means Wine Sold Here. *Dégustation Gratuite* means Free Tasting. (The English word 'disgusting' means putting you *off* your gusto; *dégustation* is linked with *goûter*, to taste, and means putting it *down* with gusto.)

Establishments exhibiting signs such as these might be small, offering only one sort of wine, and you might be received rather informally. With luck, this can lead to making friends and learning something about local life. A large establishment might be well organised for dealing with a flow of visitors: perhaps an English-speaking 'hostess', leaflets, car-stickers and a tour of the vats and the bottling machinery before one is treated to a series of small glasses. Some will be private establishments, perhaps called *Domaine de* something-or-other; a *cave coopérative* does the wine-making for a number of small local *viticulteurs* (grape-growers) and is not to be looked down on. Some fine *AOC* and *VDQS* wines come from producers' cooperatives. *Une cave*, by the way, means a cellar, literally, but most of these places are above ground. (A cave is *une caverne*.)

Vous vendez en vrac? 'Do you sell wine "loose", to be taken away in my own containers?' is an important question. If the answer is no, honour can be satisfied by buying a bottle (*une bouteille*) or two, from the small man producing high quality wine. Larger places, if they don't sell *en vrac*, may sell bottles only in half-dozens or dozens, which may not be an attractive proposition; but such places usually do their *visite* and *dégustation* exercises for the sake of public relations, and you can make them happy by asking *Vous exportez en Angleterre?* ('Do you export to Great Britain?' – Wales and Scotland are normally thought of as part of *Angleterre*) and ostentatiously making notes. Big *caves* often sell only their cheaper wines *en vrac*; these are sometimes as good as (or even the same as; see page 182) what is in the bottle with the impressive label. (*Nu*, naked, is an alternative word for *en vrac*, but usually only in written French, thus avoiding heavy-handed jocularity about selling or buying nude.)

If the answer is yes, and when one has done one's tasting, what will one take the wine away in? Not in wine-bottles; that would be like asking for a tablespoonful of beer at a pub.

Many *caves* stock containers of various kinds, at normal prices. But if you have decided that you are going to make wine-buying excursions, you will have a wider choice at the *droguerie*, and should have gone there first.

The big spherical glass *bonbonne* or carboy, with its great cork and its wicker (usually plastic nowadays) cover, is picturesque but not practical. Heavy, for one thing, especially in sizes over five litres. Choose *un jerrican* in *plastique alimentaire* (non-poisonous plastic); white plastic is usually *alimentaire*, coloured *jerricans* are for petrol, etc. It does no harm to ask the salesperson: *C'est pour le vin?'* 'Is this for wine?' Choose one with a convenient spout, often concealed under the cap. *Jerricans* are cheap; around 2 francs per litre capacity. Five litres is a convenient size, rather over a British gallon; nearly seven ordinary wine-bottles. Ten litres is all right; it will weigh just over 10 kilos when full, or 22 lb, and I cheerfully carry one in each hand for short distances, and lift one up when bottling. I would be in difficulties with anything bigger. I never go for a drive anywhere without a couple of *jerricans* in the boot in case I find a new place or two. Always be ready for a chat and a bit of *dégustation* wherever you're going.

So you have decided to lash out as a bulk buyer, spending 40p or even 50p a litre for five or more litres. Your charming young hostess (or picturesque old peasant if it's that sort of place) will write out your bill, and then get busy on another bit of paperwork. This is the *congé*, or *laisser-passer*. The point is that all wine, whether it's 10 litres in a *jerrican* or 10,000 litres in a road-tanker, has to be identifiable while it's in transit, in the hope of preventing Château Whatsit stretching its output by adding a tanker-full or two of our good Midi wine. The form states what the wine is, how much there is of it, when it left the *cave*, the registration number of the vehicle, where it is going, and when it is expected to get there. If you own a nice little vineyard in the best Burgundy area and are heading towards it with a full wine-tanker you may expect to be stopped by the police, and woe betide you if you haven't got a *congé*, or if your *congé* suggests that something fishy is under way. But no one has ever stopped my little car to ask if I've got a *jerrican* of plonk. However, regulations are regulations; they write out my *congé*, and I'm supposed to keep it until I get the wine home.

If you are going to take more than your duty-free allowance of wine back to Britain, the Customs officers at British ports know about these *congés*, and if you show one to them you may save a certain amount of fuss and bother.

It all sounds rather fearsome, but it's quite painless really, and takes only a moment (or, in the right circumstances and with the right person, is the basis and excuse for a prolonged gossip on the congenial subject of oneself).

Wine keeps well in plastic for two or three months, but not longer. But it won't keep at all in a partially empty container; if you pour off a litre from your *jerrican* you must bottle the rest. As you will have started your holiday by buying your wine at the supermarket, you should have in your *gîte* or tent enough bottles for a *jerrican* (another argument in favour of the small five-litre size). At the *droguerie* you should have bought a few *bouchons coniques*, corks with one end smaller than the other. Don't get the ordinary *bouchons cylindriques*: you need a special instrument for getting these in, and you have to boil them first, to soften them. A *bouchon conique* is not good enough if you're laying the wine down for your grandchildren, but it goes in easily. A cheap plastic funnel (*un entonnoir*) can be got at the *droguerie* too.

Rinse your *jerrican* out. A spoonful of wine left at the bottom will turn to vinegar; if you put the next lot of wine on top of it you will have to drink it quickly or it will be vinegar too. Home wine-makers know about sterilising with a sodium metabisulphite solution; *sulfite* comes from the *droguerie*, and if you are suspicious about the interior of your *jerricans* you can always rinse with a solution.

As I said earlier, *vins de table* and *vins de pays* are sold with an indication of their alcoholic strength. In ten years of buying wine *en vrac* every three weeks I have only once had some wine go *piqué* (vinegary) on me, and that was a weakish (10°) sample. Friends of mine take 80 litres of robust 13° local red wine home to Scotland every year and have never been disappointed.

Eighty litres, you say? Easy enough, if you take it *en vrac* and are not blessed with numerous offspring or can make the offspring shove up a bit. A case of six normal wine-bottles (a total of 4½ litres) measures 12½″ × 7″ × 10″, or 875 cubic inches, or 0.5 cubic foot, and weighs a lot because of the glass. My plastic 10-litre *jerrican* weighs little, and measures 15″ (right up to the top of the handle) × 10½″ × 5″, or 787 cubic inches, or 0.46 cubic foot: well over twice as much wine in less space. Eight of those take up just over 3½ cubic feet; total weight, a fraction over 80 kilos, or around 13 stone; no more than a good-sized mother-in-law. The Customs allow some of this to pass duty-free (the allowance changes from time to time – check as you leave England, to know what your bill will be on your return). My friends pay up on the rest and find it a bargain. Back in sunny Scotland they give a bottling party (*dégustation gratuite* all round).

THE VOCABULARY OF WINE-TASTING
At the Coarse French level, much can be done – indeed, all that is necessary – with a graduated series of ejaculations. *Hmmm!, aah!, bon!, très bon!* and *très très bon!* are quite enough

to give pleasure to the person who is letting you taste samples of his wines, especially when accompanied with suitably judicious facial contortions. Kissing the fingers of one's right hand and then waving them high in the air should perhaps be left to the natives.

Virtuosi can have fun, and perhaps impress the listener, with a selection of the following terms.

Before tasting, one might talk about:

le cépage: the variety of grape (many wines include several *cépages*).

le raisin: the grape. (*Une grappe* is a bunch of grapes; a currant or raisin is a *raisin sec,* a dried grape.)

le cru: an inclusive descriptive word for a particular wine, encompassing the vineyard, its soil characteristics, the *cépage,* the year, the microclimate . . . so one can use it as a synonym for a wine – *C'est un cru intéressant! Quel cru!*

Waving the stuff around in the glass and holding it up to the light, one can remark on its agreeable colour. The word *la robe* is more *distinguée* than *la couleur* for such comments . . . (*Belle robe! Si claire, si vive!*).

One will then sniff it. Only the better wines have much of a perfume. If *une odeur agréable* can be detected, *le parfum* or *l'arôme* (m.) will do.

le bouquet is (by purists) reserved for old wines. If you know the wine to be last year's (therefore young), and it has a pleasant smell, you will get high marks from those who go in for this sort of word-play if you say something like *Quel arôme! Ça donnera un bouquet magnifique plus tard!*

Drink it. The spitting-out routine is only for professionals who spend the whole day on the job, or if you are at some noble Bordeaux *château* and are deliberately experiencing a wine too young to be drinkable, offered in the belief that you will be able to detect signs of future greatness.

If it seems full-bodied hefty stuff:

capiteux: powerful, alcoholic, goes to the head.

charnu: mouth-filling; lots of body.

    charpenté: strong, well-balanced.

    le coeur: a noun, to replace the above adjectives. *Quel coeur!*

    étoffé: much as above. A wine that is *étoffé* keeps well.

    généreux: as above.

    la mâche: a wine has *de la mâche* when it has the above qualities; you could almost *mâcher* (chew) it. Good word for decent plonk of 12° or 13°: *il a de la mâche, ce vin!*

    rond, and especially *velouté,* are nice adjectives for smoother wines of this type.

On the other hand, for light wines we have:

    frais, for an unassuming young specimen.

    fruité, also for a young fresh wine. This is what Beaujolais *nouveau*, or any other drinkable new wine, should be.

    délicat: little acidity, light colour.

    élégant: not much *mâche,* but goes down nicely.

    gouleyant: highly quaffable in large quantities.

    léger: just light; not a real compliment.

    souple: same as *gouleyant*, if you're running out of words.

    tendre: more complimentary than *léger*.

The above list does not cater for Masters of Wine, or for frank judgements of inferior products; it should be regarded as an aid to human relationships.

Chapter 20

Beer

Campaigners for Real Ale have no chance, in France, of finding a tankard of best bitter, drawn from the wood and served with a chunk of mature Cheddar and a couple of nice pickled onions. But a cool glass of lager-type beer is often welcome, and easily found at any time of the day.

The standard type of French beer comes in small non-returnable bottles. They hold 25cl, or a scant half pint. Kronenbourg, Slavia, Kanterbräu, "33", Mutzig and the Belgian Stella Artois are well-known makes. They cost, in shops but not in cafés, about a third of what one would pay in Britain, and provide a thirst-quenching and moderately fizzy glassful. Harmless, too; the average Frenchman considers beer a non-alcoholic drink, and the notion that determined people might drink several glasses, one after the other, strikes him as bizarre. They are on sale in *épiceries*, supermarkets and hypermarkets, usually in packs of six to twenty-four bottles.

Some of these makes, and a few others such as Valstar, can be bought in returnable litre bottles. These big bottles, less the deposit, cost about twice the price of the little bottles, but hold four times as much. A good bargain for the camper and the *gîte*-dweller. They have screw tops, so a partly consumed bottle can go in the fridge or the cold-box until next time. A word of warning: some shops keep them upright, others lying down. Buy the latter, when you can. The factory may have failed to screw the top on firmly enough. In a horizontal bottle the modest gas pressure forces some of the beer out, neighbouring bottles get sticky, one can see that the bottle isn't quite full, and one doesn't put it in one's trolley. Upright, however, the gas just escapes, and one eventually opens a full bottle of flat beer. It doesn't often happen, but once I had two flat bottles out of four; I was gravely disgruntled, as I do look forward to a dew-misted glass of Valstar for my midsummer elevenses (at under 10p, too).

Prices are variable from shop to shop. I do hope that readers will take an interest in the small shopkeeper, and let her or him take an interest in them; but for factory-made products such as beer, the big outlets are usually much cheaper. At our nearest village shop a litre bottle of Valstar costs 40 per cent more than at the hypermarket (where they keep them lying down, too). As so often in France, it pays to look around, even in the same hypermarket: 'special offer' prices can be lower than those for the same goods on a different shelf.

Returning the empties: there is no need to return your empty litre beer bottles (litre wine and lemonade bottles too) to the particular shop you got them from. Any place selling similar bottles will do. In the small shop you just hand in your old bottle as you buy the new one. But in many supermarkets there is a special place where empties are handed in. This sort of returnable deposit is called a *consigne*, so you look out for a notice saying *bouteilles consignées* or *verre consigné* or *reprise de bouteilles*.

J'ai des bouteilles consignées – qu'est-ce que je dois en faire?: 'I've got some bottles with a deposit on them; what am I supposed to do with them?'

They will give you your money in cash, or a chit for use at the check-out.

In cafés, if you just ask for '*une bière*', you will probably get one of the standard 25cl bottles of light beer; or perhaps – if it is where the smart set go, or if you look like a rich foreigner – it will be an up-market bottle. In any case you will pay from three to five times the 'off-licence' price. I prefer going to a biggish café when I want to sit in the shade for half an hour with a glass of beer – they will have it in keg (*sous pression* – under pressure). Ask for *une pression* ('a glass of draught lager'), and you will get 25cl at the right temperature, at about what you would pay in a British pub.

In big towns there may be a specialist café for beer enthusiasts, where a variety of imported brews may be had, a round of some of which might cost as much as a bottle of champagne. Here too one might see enormous tankards holding as much as a litre, called by fancy names such as *une sérieuse, une distinguée, une masse*. . . People quaffing from these are usually tourists, and the passing *bourgeoisie* shudder faintly.

Beer in restaurants: as in cafés, but a fraction dearer. *Not* a cheaper alternative to the *vin de pays*.

Chapter 21

The language

If one's last memories of learning French are connected with written examinations, perhaps with a small oral test thrown in, a change of attitude is needed. In exams (and to a large extent at school generally) one must try to avoid mistakes; play safe; don't risk putting a foot wrong and getting marks lopped off. In 'real' life, on the other hand, the only mistake that matters is a failure in communication. Genders, for example: at O and A level, you lose a mark if you get one wrong, but in practice it is better to know a lot of nouns than to be a gender-expert. Highly complex thoughts can be expressed with just the simple conjunctions *et, mais* and *si*; no need to dredge up from the recesses of the memory lists of elegant written-style conjunctions that may, or may not, according to subtle distinctions, take the subjunctive. Full marks for getting the meaning across, *somehow*, with suitable gestures and even an English word or two (basic, and clearly pronounced); your Frenchman will come halfway to meet you.

Pronunciation

Some aspects of pronunciation are worth taking very serious-ly, or one will fail to communicate. Other aspects are less important. In this section an attempt is made to distinguish both. Some teachers, most examining boards and almost all helpful French friends have overall perfection in mind; this leads to dispersal of effort if communication is the aim.

Anyone who wants to disguise himself as a native French-man needs long sessions with experts in phonetics and voice production. If there are any agents of the British Intelligence Service deceiving the French counter-espionage squad in this way, they probably had a French aunt or two. For all other purposes, there is nothing wrong with an English accent, if your French can be understood painlessly at the first attempt. In fact the French quite like it, just as we accept Scottish, American or French accents (especially French, when the speaker is a charming film star).

Of all the vowel-sounds and consonant-sounds of French (I am choosing my words carefully; I am not talking about spelling problems or about rhythm and stress) there is only one that the English-speaker must take serious trouble with, and that is the *u* sound (represented by [y] in the International Phonetic Alphabet) as in *la rue*. All the other sounds of French, if produced in an 'English' way, will be accepted by French hearers as odd but understandable pronunciations.

An example: if anybody starts bullying you about the French R, and you don't want to be bothered because you've got something better to do (like mugging up a whole lot of useful nouns, or going fishing in a mountain stream), just blind him with science and tell him that the difference isn't phonemic. The French hear lots of different R versions, from the lovely (when purred by a beautiful girl) uvular Parisian one to the almost-Scottish rolled one from Perpignan, not forgetting the low-life Parisian version – really a glottal stop, like a Cockney or a Glaswegian T in 'a bottle of dirty water'. Your English R is easily understood as just another version.

With *rue*, you *must* get the vowel right, in a totally French way; but the consonant is just an optional extra.

Stress and rhythm

Getting the stress wrong can lead to failure in communication. I once took a long time to grasp which English town a Dutch friend was talking about: he called it Ex*eter* instead of *Ex*eter (and he had trouble finding the lav*a*tory). And last year I had to examine a foreign student who kept going on about 'arrears'; I was puzzled until he used the word in a context that showed he had *areas* in mind.

Luckily French is much easier than English in this respect. In any group of syllables the stress is roughly equal on each and every syllable, but with a slight stress on the last one. So a Frenchman may have problems in getting to Har*rods* or Simp*sons* if that is what he calls them; Lou Whisker Roll, I was told, wrote *Alice in Wonderland*.

So: a 2-syllable group (*merci*) goes ti-TA;
  a 3-syllable group (*Avignon*) goes ti-ti-TA;
  a 4-syllable group (*Bonjour monsieur*) goes ti-ti-ti-TA;
  and a 5-syllable group (*le Mont-Saint-Michel*) goes ti-ti-ti-ti-TA.

Easy but important. Let me re-emphasise the difference. Compare the English words photograph and photography. Not only does the stressed syllable shift; the shift changes all the spoken vowels. With *photographe* and *photographie* we go from ti-ti-Ta to ti-ti-ti-TA, but the vowels stay unchanged. Simple. (*Un photographe* is a photographer, and *une photographie* is a photo – *une photo* for short – but that's another matter.)

Intonation, or melody

There won't be many groups of more than five syllables; one has to pause to breathe or think. The syllables in the group will be delivered all on one note except the last one. If you have finished your sentence, the last syllable is about a semi-tone lower. If you haven't finished, it will be about a semi-tone higher.

There is one useful exception, for questions. Old-fashioned French courses, and those concerned mainly with the written language, suggest that there are two equally good ways of turning a statement (*vous êtes anglais*) into a question:

with inversion: *êtes-vous anglais?*

or with *est-ce que: est-ce que vous êtes anglais?*

Then they add the complication that if the subject is a noun rather than a pronoun (statement: *Fred est anglais*), inversion has to be done with an inserted pronoun; NOT *est Fred anglais?* but

Fred est-il anglais?

or the easier uninverted *est-ce que Fred est anglais?*

That is all very well, but it ignores the fact that in SPOKEN French, 95 per cent of questions are made much more simply (almost nobody would ever SAY *Fred est-il anglais?*). One just uses the statement form with a rising tune instead of a falling one. Thus:

vous êtes anglais?

Fred est anglais?

with the last syllable going up a semi-tone. Absolutely no problem. It will not do for written French, but it is good spoken French.

(The main use of the *est-ce que* form, which is easy too, is for emphasis or to gain thinking-time. If one says *est-ce que* firmly, and pauses, it indicates 'I am going to ask you a question; pay attention and wait for it.')

Plenty of listening is helpful. Turn on the radio and let the noise of French speech flow over you, even if you are a beginner and can't understand a word. One can do it in the car in England, tuned in to a French station: pay attention to the road, letting the sounds, rhythms and tunes of spoken French soak into the subconscious.

Spelling

As I have implied, the pronunciation of French is fairly simple and straightforward. There is no grave problem in identifying

197

the noises the natives make, nor in producing equivalent noises in such a manner as to be easily understood. People who say that French pronunciation is difficult will usually be found to be talking not about pronunciation but about spelling.

It is only too true that French spelling bristles with difficulties (not as much as English, but more than, say, Italian) and that the difference between the written and the spoken language is huge. It is part of the business of a properly thought-out course (in the classroom or in print backed up by cassettes) to help here. But the point for someone mainly interested in the spoken language is this: he must believe that the *real* word or phrase or sentence is the one he hears spoken. Seeing what it looks like when written is a secondary (and distracting) matter. (If he gets letters from ordinary French people, neither university educated nor secretaries, he will have ample opportunity to see it wrongly spelt, which is why it is sometimes like drawing teeth to get a letter out of the French: they have guilt feelings about the trickier spelling rules, they feel they *ought* to know them. . . .) It is perverse that our A-levellists spell French better than French youngsters, while any French seven-year-old can out-perform them in spoken communication. The cart has come before the horse, and even with language laboratories and so forth the mechanics of the classroom and of examining *en masse* keep the cart in front.

The ideal is therefore to meet new words and phrases first of all in speech; commit them to one's aural memory; and only then (if at all) to concern oneself with how they are spelt. This is easier said than done, even if one is in France and living with the French: highly literate people (and my reader is a highly literate person, or he would not have got this far) do like to see it in writing. But certainly, until one is quite sure that one has mastered the technique of turning print into speech, one should not try to commit new material to memory unless one has heard it; in default of that, and if one is in earnest about improving one's performance in two-way communication, it is worthwhile using dictionaries, phrase books and courses that give the pronunciation in the International Phonetic Alphabet.

This is much more efficient than the 'zher swee onglay' sort of thing. It takes a couple of hours' study, including some practice with a French speaker (or a cassette) to learn to 'read' it, but the pay-off is considerable. (It would take much longer to learn to write down the sounds one hears, in the IPA, but that would be a waste of effort for all practical purposes; one needs only to be able to identify the symbols.)

Dictionaries

Avoid perfectionism. A pocket French-English/English-French dictionary does a good job, if one takes precautions. I have the great Harrap four-volume dictionary, each volume weighing a ton and costing a bomb. This is wonderful for professional translators; I often understand something in French perfectly but can't think how on earth one can say it in English – the big dictionary helps. But I'm not usually interested in knowing that *un estradiot* is a stradiot, *un flanquis* a saltire couped, or *flavopurpurine* flavopurpurin.

Precautions: if one is at Coarse level or below, the pocket dictionary works well enough (if one has seen the word written) in the French-English direction, because one knows the English words; but not the other way round, if that is the first time one meets the French words. There are not enough explanations. Look at it from your French opposite number's point of view. He goes to an English garage because he wants *une bougie*. He looks it up in a little dictionary: 'candle, sparking-plug'. If both those words mean *une bougie*, they mean the same thing . . . which should he choose? How can he know? Whereas you, if told that your car needed a new set of *bougies*, would not think of going to *la droguerie* for candles: you see at once which is the right translation in the context. Working from English to French is harder. Sticking to plugs, there are all sorts: plugs for the bath (*la bonde* and other words), two-pin and three-pin plugs (*la fiche*), wall-plugs to stick them in (*la prise de courant*) and even plugs of tobacco (*la chique*). A small dictionary will give you some of these, usually

199

without any help in choosing, so that it looks as though you might as well use any.

In other words, little dictionaries are fine as aids to understanding a foreign language, but they are dangerous if one uses them over-confidently to invent expressions in the foreign language. Two more examples: an English schoolboy wrote *le marc de l'école*. *L'école* is the school, *le marc* is residue after something has been fermented, brewed, etc. It turned out that he meant the school grounds. Well, yes, *le marc de café* is coffee-grounds. . . . I saw on a translated French menu 'Holy James shell'. Indeed, *saint* is holy, *Jacques* is James, and *coquille* is shell, but *une coquille Saint-Jacques* is a scallop.

The next step is to buy a French dictionary, and I mean a French one. *Le Petit Larousse Illustré* is excellent, has pictures and diagrams, and is cheap at the price. Thus you get a labelled diagram of a motor-car. If you are wondering whether it is a *bonde*, a *fiche*, a *prise* or a *chique* that you want, each is explained in simple language. (I've just looked up *estradiot* in it – *now* I know what it means. Knowing that it was 'stradiot' in English didn't help at all. It turns out that this is the only time in my life I shall ever use either word, but you see what I mean.) Nothing as good as *Le Petit Larousse* exists for the English language, unfortunately for French pupils learning our lingo.

A note on the alphabet. In crudely Coarse pronunciation the names of the letters are:

A: ah	B: bay	C: say	D: day
E: this may be called 'er' (as in *le*) or 'eh' (as in *café*)	F: eff	G: zhay (jay without the d sound at the beginning)	H: arsh
I: ee	J: zhee	K: kah	L: el
M: em	N: en	O: oh	P: pay
Q: ku (French u)	R: air	S: ess	T: tay
U: French u	V: vay	W: doobl vay	X: ix
Y: ee-grec	Z: zed		

F, L, M, N, O, S and Z are roughly as in English. B, C, D, H, K, P, Q (if you've got the u), T, U (again), V, W, X and Y are different but no problem. The rest present traps, going from one language or the other. If you're called Rogers and spell your name with the English alphabet, you may find yourself appearing as Mr Aojias. 'Double', when spelling a word, is *deux*. Therefore, Cobb is spelled *C, O, deux B*.

Numbers

Shopkeepers and so forth are always willing to jot down the amount you have to pay. (French handwritten figures are somewhat different from what one is used to. The figure 1 can look like an A without a bar, because it starts with an up stroke; therefore *cross your sevens* or they may be taken for ones.)

Dix soixante-six (ten sixty-six) is not a date. It is part of a telephone number. French telephone numbers are always given in pairs, like English dates. As part of a phone number, 1234 appears as 12 34 and is *douze, trente-quatre*, not *un deux trois quatre*; if you give it as *un deux trois quatre* you will be understood, but *they* won't give it to you like that.

Dates are said in full. 1066 is *mil soixante six*, 1939 is *mil neuf cent trente-neuf*. (*Mille* is a thousand, but it is spelt *mil* in dates only. The sound is the same, and nine Frenchmen out of ten are muddled about this; so if you follow my advice about spelling, you won't worry about it at all. I would really have liked to write *mille* in the date above, like all my neighbours, but I suffer from inhibitions.)

'One franc, fifty centimes' is written F1,50 or 1,50 f.

'Three point one four two' is 3,142, 'point' being *virgule*, comma. 'Three thousand one hundred and forty-two' is 3.142, the full-stop being on the line.

When it comes to prices, the French have still, after a quarter of a century, not wholly got used to new francs. You will sometimes hear older people call F1,50 *cent cinquante francs* (a hundred and fifty . . .) instead of *un franc cinquante*.

This is not much of a problem, though. If your bill seems about a hundred times more than you bargained for, any international noise of amazement will produce a translation from *anciens francs* into *nouveaux francs*. With house prices, old francs die hard. This is because *un million*, a million old francs – 10,000 new ones, or getting on for £1000 – is such a useful unit. Some estate agents have taken to calling this sum *une unité* (a unit), but most people, when buying or selling houses, stick to the old *million*.

People who won't speak a word of French have a wonderful time, and they do good to the natives, all of whom learn some English at school these days. Speak English loud and clear, and don't take *non* for an answer. They are just bashful. (Of course, if you can be firm it follows that you aren't bashful, and everyone learns French these days.)

Misleading words

Here is a small collection of words that cause problems. They are mostly *faux amis* ('false friends'), looking like English words but meaning something different. They can cause misunderstandings when seen or heard in French; Frenchmen may use the look-alike English word wrongly when speaking English.

GENERAL

accuser réception – to acknowledge receipt (of a letter, etc.).

actuellement – not 'actually' but 'at the present time'; similarly *actuel*: present, current.

ancien – when before the noun, not 'old' but 'former'; your *ancien mari* (ex-husband) could be younger than your *mari actuel*.

appoint (m.): *faire l'appoint* – to pay the exact amount; 'no change given'.

aspic (m.) – not only aspic jelly, but also French lavender.

assister – can mean to help, though usually in a financial sense (in receipt of public funds; *enfants assistés* – children in care) but more usually it means 'to be present'. *Venez assister* – come and take part (no suggestion of helping). *L'assistance* can mean the people present. (To help – *aider*.)

attendre – to wait for.

avertissement (m.) – a warning. An advertisement is *une annonce*.

baskets (m.) – shoes for basketball, sneakers (popular leisure shoes for the young). *Lâche-moi les baskets* (slang) – stop bothering me.

brassière (f.) – in the plural, shoulder-straps for a rucksack. Not the item of underwear, which is *un soutien-gorge*.

car (m.) short for *autocar* – motor coach. A private car is *une voiture de tourisme*.

cette nuit – usually means *last* night (unless the context makes it clear that tonight is meant). *J'ai bien dormi cette nuit* – I slept well last night. Use *ce soir* for tonight: *on va au cinéma ce soir* – we're going to the cinema tonight. *La nuit* ends at dawn; until the small hours of the morning – *jusqu'à une heure avancée de la nuit*.

chicorée (f.) is endive (*c. frisée* – curly-leaved e., *c. scarole* – plain-leaved endive). *Endive* (f.), however, is chicory. A fine muddle, especially as *chicorée* means chicory when the roots are roasted for stretching coffee.

chiffon (m.) – a cleaning rag.

chouette! (slang) – nice, super.

commander – to order (in a restaurant: *J'ai commandé un bifteck*). *Ordonner* means to arrange things in order (of size, for example).

composter – to date-stamp railway tickets, etc.

correspondance (f.) – correspondence, but also connection (between trains, flights, etc.). *Correspondance pour —— –* change (trains, etc.) for ——

eventuel, eventuellement – not eventual or eventually, but 'if the occasion arises'. *Les accidents eventuels pendant vos vacances* are the accidents that might perhaps occur during your holidays.

extra – short for *extraordinaire* (colloquial) – good. *Le bifteck est extra* does not mean that you have to pay extra for it; it is jolly good. An extra charge is *un supplément*.

foot (m.) – football (soccer).

grappe (f.) – a bunch (e.g. of grapes). A grape is *un raisin*.

hôtel (m.) – hotel, but also large town house (the aristocracy had *châteaux* in the country and *hôtels* in town); and some kinds of public building (*hôtel de ville* – town hall; *hôtel de police* – police HQ).

important – important, but also simply big. If you have *des bagages importants* you have a lot of heavy luggage.

incessamment – can mean unceasingly, but more usually it means immediately. *J'arriverai incessamment* – I'll be along in a moment.

intoxication (f.) – poisoning. If you have eaten something that disagrees with you, you are *intoxiqué*. But if you are drunk, you are *ivre*, not *intoxiqué*.

laurier (m.) – laurel, strictly speaking. But laurel leaves are poisonous. When a recipe says add *une feuille de laurier* it means a bay leaf (bay tree – *laurier-sauce*).

location (f.) – hiring, renting. *Location de voitures* – car hire. To rent – *louer*; the hirer or tenant is *le locataire*.

milliard (m.) – a thousand million (the American billion).

mince – thin. To mince – *hacher*. *Un émincé de* —— – a thin slice of —— (seen usually on menus).

monnaie (f.) – change. *Contrôlez votre monnaie* – check your change. Money is *l'argent* (m.).

perception (f.) – collection of taxes and certain other charges. *Le percepteur* is the tax-collector.

permanence (f.) – as well as the English meaning, *une permanence* can also be loosely used to mean staff or service on duty: *permanence à 1800 h.* – someone will open the office at six; *je suis de permanence* – I'm on duty.

ponctuel – as well as punctual, this can mean at irregular points of time. *Des visites ponctuelles* – visits from time to time and at any time.

pull (m.) – pullover.

rentable – profitable (nothing necessarily to do with available for hire).

slip (m.) – briefs, men's underpants.

société (f.) – society, but also commercial company. *SARL – société anonyme à responsibilité limitée* – Ltd.

sweat (m.) – short for *sweat-shirt*, sometimes seen as *sweet-shirt*.

taxe (f.) – can mean tax, but more commonly official price; *taxes postales, taxes téléphoniques* – postal rates, telephone charges.

terrible – loosely and colloquially, means amazingly good. *Des prix terribles* – astounding bargain prices. *Ce bifteck n'est pas terrible* – this steak isn't much good.

usé – worn out. A used car (for sale) is *une voiture d'occasion*; *une voiture usée* is fit only for the scrap-heap.

WORDS ABOUT PEOPLE

un Alsacien – an inhabitant of Alsace. An Alsatian (dog) is *un berger allemand* – a German shepherd.

Anglais(e), Angleterre – colloquially, Scotland (*L'Écosse*) and Wales (*le Pays de Galles*) are districts of *l'Angleterre*. An Aberdonian in kilt and sporran is easily identifiable as *un Anglais*.

Anglo-saxon(ne) – universally used to mean English-speaking; nothing to do with King Alfred or Beowulf. If you were born in the Bronx of mixed Chinese, Negro, Red Indian and Russian ancestry you are *un Anglo-saxon*, and a French punk wearing a T-shirt labelled Massachusetts Institute of Technology listening to the Stranglers on his *walkman* is an example of the deplorable *impérialisme cultural anglo-saxon*. The *Rainbow Warrior* affair taught the French a lot about *la justice anglo-saxonne*.

blesser – to wound. *Les blessés* – the wounded. To bless – *bénir*.

fatigué – colloquially used instead of *malade*; ill, poorly.

génial – *un homme génial* is a genius; he may not be genial or congenial.

malice (f.), *malicieux* – can mean what they look like, but more usually smart(ness), acute(ness), clever(ness). Dennis the Menace — *Denis la Malice*.

malin, maligne — except in medicine (*une tumeur maligne* or *bénigne*) the 'bad' meaning is archaic. It normally means clever. *Ce n'était pas très malin* — That wasn't very bright, was it?

parent (m.) — *vos parents* are your relations, not just your parents (except when the context makes the latter meaning clear). *Mon plus proche parent* — my next of kin.

patron (m.) — boss. If you go to a café you are *un client*; the owner or manager is *le patron*.

sein (m.) — a breast, normally occurring as one of a pair; when the French are trying to purge themselves of *le franglais* they talk of *seins nus* instead of *le topless*. Mentioned here because it can also be a womb (literally or figuratively), where the soon-to-be-born child, or revolution, or bright idea is in hiding. French ladies thus boast three *seins*. *Au sein de l'hexagone* just means 'in France'.

sensible — not 'sensible' (which is *raisonnable*) but 'sensitive'. *Un coeur sensible* — a tender heart.

sérieux — not so much 'serious' as genuine, earnest, responsible. At *un restaurant sérieux* they know their job. A serious illness is *une maladie grave*.

spirituel — not so much 'spiritual' as witty, amusing.

sympathique (slang: *sympa*) — nice. *Un type sympa* — a nice chap. Can be used of things as well as people; *un film sympa* is *chouette*.

A last word

The object of the exercise is to have a good time. *Amusez-vous bien!* The French will go most of the way to help you do this, especially if it looks as though you share some of their convictions about what constitutes the good life.

Sophie and I would be delighted to hear of your experiences, and to know what you think of this book. Write to us care of the publisher. We do answer letters.

Bonnes vacances!

Bon retour!

Useful addresses

Air France
158 New Bond Street
LONDON W1Y 0AY

Agence Nationale Pour L'Information Touristique (ANIT)
8 avenue de l'Opéra
75001 PARIS
France

French National Tourist Office (FNTO)
178 Piccadilly
LONDON W1V 0AL

French Railways (SNCF)
179 Piccadilly
LONDON W1V 0BA

Gîtes de France
178 Piccadilly
LONDON W1V 0AL

Office de Tourisme de Paris
127 avenue des Champs-Élysées
75008 PARIS
France

Consuls:

PARIS DISTRICT
British Embassy
35 rue de Faubourg St Honoré
75383 PARIS Cedex 08. Tel. 42 66 91 42

BORDEAUX DISTRICT
British Consulate General
15 Cours de Verdun
33081 BORDEAUX Cedex. Tel. 56 52 28 35

LILLE DISTRICT
British Consulate General
11 Square Dutilleul
59800 LILLE Tel. 20 57 87 90

LYONS DISTRICT
British Consulate General
24 rue Childebert
69288 LYON Cedex 1. Tel. 78 37 59 67

MARSEILLES DISTRICT
British Consulate General
24 Avenue du Prado
13006 MARSEILLE Tel. 91 53 43 32, 91 37 66 95

Honorary Consuls:

British Consulate at the following addresses:

c/o British Railways, Gare Maritime, BP 27,
62201 BOULOGNE-SUR-MER Cedex.
Tel. 21 30 25 11

Ferry Terminal Building, Port of Calais, 62101 CALAIS.
Tel. 21 96 33 76

Townsend Thoresen, Gare Maritime, 50101 CHERBOURG.
Tel. 33 44 20 13

'La Hulotte', 8 Avenue de la Libération, 35800 DINARD.
Tel. 99 46 26 64

L. Dewulf, Cailleret & Fils, 11 rue des Arbres, BP 1502, 59383
DUNKERQUE. Tel. 28 66 11 98

9 quai George V, 76600 LE HAVRE.
Tel. 35 42 27 47

BP 264, 6 rue Lafayette, 44009 NANTES Cedex.
Tel. 40 48 57 47

11 rue Paradis, 06000 NICE. Tel. 93 82 32 04

10 rue Grande des Fabriques, 66000 PERPIGNAN.
Tel. 68 34 56 99

(near TOULOUSE) British Aerospace Offices, c/o Airbus
Industrie, 2 ave Lucien Servanty, 31700 BLAGNAC.
Tel. 61 71 00 10, 61 93 35 60

Select bibliography

Hotels and restaurants

The red Michelin guide, France is published annually, appearing in the spring. Satisfactory for those who do not read French. Obtainable everywhere in France, and in many bookshops in Britain.

Le Guide Gault Millau France appears annually in December, dated the following year. Critical descriptions in French of over 5000 establishments. A good reading knowledge of French is required. Obtainable everywhere in France, and in specialist British bookshops (at a much higher price, usually, unlike Michelin).

The Best of France, Gault Millau will be published in England in 1986. A selection, in English, of about half the entries in the main French edition. Useful for those who do not read French. It is not clear whether it will be revised annually; if not, people with a moderate amount of French will prefer the current year's French edition.

Logis et Auberges de France. Published annually. No reading knowledge of French required. Free from FNTO (French National Tourist Office) or for about 30 francs at French bookshops.

Relais et Châteaux. Published annually. Almost no French required. Free from FNTO.

English books recommending hotels and restaurants can be useful *in the year of publication;* less reliable thereafter, especially if they list fewer than a thousand establishments (the 'GB-plate ghetto' risk).

Other matters

Michelin Camping Caravanning, France. Published annually. No French needed (symbols, four-language glossary). Obtainable almost everywhere in France; specialist bookshops in Britain.

Stations Vertes guide. Good knowledge of French required. See page 30 for how to obtain.

Living in France Today, Philip Holland, published by Hale, 1985 edition. For settlers.

For settlers in Paris, *Practically Yours, Paris and France* is published by UNESCO Community Service, 7 place de Fontenoy, 75700 Paris. It is written for English-speaking Unesco employees, but is available — and useful — to 'outsiders'. Obtainable at the place de Fontenoy office, and by post from there (enquire for price).

The Traveller in France, published annually, free and post free, from FNTO.

General and regional guides — Blue, Companion, Fodor,

Nagel, Shell and many others — are numerous and various. One's man's cherished guide is another man's crashing bore. See Chapter 2. (A more attractive but less detailed guide to Paris than the green Michelin English-language one is *A Paris* (Visa/Hachette, 1985) but at the moment it is available only in French.)

Food and Cookery: books mentioned in the text

Ann Barr and Paul Levy, *'Harpers & Queen' Official Foodie Handbook*, Ebury Press, 1984. Mainly for fun, but with a stratum of good sense.

Elizabeth David, *French Provincial Cooking*, Penguin, 1970.

Alan Davidson, *Mediterranean Seafood*, Penguin, 1972.

Jane Grigson, *Charcuterie and French Pork Cookery*, Penguin, 1970.

Jane Grigson, *Vegetable Book*, Penguin, 1980.

Index